כַּפָּהּ, פָּרְשָׂה לֶעָנִי; וְיָדֶיהָ, שִׁלְּחָה לָאֶבְיוֹן

kappah paresah le'ani; veyadeiha, shillechah la'evyon

She stretcheth out her hand to the poor; yea, she reacheth forth her hands to the needy.

לֹא-תִירָא לְבֵיתָהּ מִשָּׁלֶג: כִּי כָל-בֵּיתָהּ, לָבֻשׁ שָׁנִים

lo-tira leveitah mishaleg; ki chol-beitah, lavush shanim

She is not afraid of the snow for her household; for all her household are clothed with scarlet.

מַרְבַדִּים עָשְׂתָה-לָּהּ; שֵׁשׁ וְאַרְגָּמָן לְבוּשָׁהּ

marvaddim asetah-lah; shesh ve'argaman levushah

She maketh for herself coverlets; her clothing is fine linen and purple.

נוֹדָע בַּשְּׁעָרִים בַּעְלָהּ; בְּשִׁבְתּוֹ, עִם-זִקְנֵי-אָרֶץ

noda bashe'arim ba'lah; beshivto, im-ziknei-'aretz

Her husband is known in the gates, when he sitteth among the elders of the land.

סָדִין עָשְׂתָה, וַתִּמְכֹּר; וַחֲגוֹר, נָתְנָה לַכְּנַעֲנִי

sadin asetah vattimkor; vachagor, natenah lakkena'ni

She maketh linen garments and selleth them; and delivereth girdles unto the merchant.

עֹז-וְהָדָר לְבוּשָׁהּ; וַתִּשְׂחַק, לְיוֹם אַחֲרוֹן

'oz-vehadar levushah; vattischak, leyom acharon

Strength and dignity are her clothing; and she laugheth at the time to come.

פִּיהָ, פָּתְחָה בְחָכְמָה; וְתוֹרַת חֶסֶד, עַל-לְשׁוֹנָהּ

piha patechah vechochmah; vetorat-chesed, al-leshonah

She openeth her mouth with wisdom; and the law of kindness is on her tongue.

צוֹפִיָּה, הֲלִיכוֹת בֵּיתָהּ; וְלֶחֶם עַצְלוּת, לֹא תֹאכֵל

tzofiyah halichot beitah; velechem atzlut, lo tochel

She looketh well to the ways of her household, and eateth not the bread of idleness.

קָמוּ בָנֶיהָ, וַיְאַשְּׁרוּהָ; בַּעְלָהּ, וַיְהַלְלָהּ

kamu vaneiha vay'asheruha; ba'lah, vayhalelah

Her children rise up, and call her blessed; her husband also, and he praiseth her:

רַבּוֹת בָּנוֹת, עָשׂוּ חָיִל; וְאַתְּ, עָלִית עַל-כֻּלָּנָה

rabbot banot asu chayil; ve'at, alit al-kullanah

'Many daughters have done valiantly, but thou excellest them all.'

שֶׁקֶר הַחֵן, וְהֶבֶל הַיֹּפִי: אִשָּׁה יִרְאַת-יְהוָה, הִיא תִתְהַלָּל

sheker hachen vehevel hayofi; ishah yir'at-hashem hi tit'hallal

Grace is deceitful, and beauty is vain; but a woman that feareth the LORD, she shall be praised.

תְּנוּ-לָהּ, מִפְּרִי יָדֶיהָ; וִיהַלְלוּהָ בַשְּׁעָרִים מַעֲשֶׂיהָ

tenu-lah mipperi yadeiha; viyhaleluha vashe'arim ma'aseiha

Give her of the fruit of her hands; and let her works praise her in the gates.

פְּתַח-פִּיךָ לְאִלֵּם; אֶל-דִּין, כָּל-בְּנֵי חֲלוֹף

petach-picha le'illem; el-din, kol-benei chalof

Open thy mouth for the dumb, in the cause of all such as are appointed to destruction.

פְּתַח-פִּיךָ שְׁפָט-צֶדֶק; וְדִין, עָנִי וְאֶבְיוֹן

petach-picha shefat-tzedek; vedin, ani ve'evyon

Open thy mouth, judge righteously, and plead the cause of the poor and needy.

אֵשֶׁת-חַיִל, מִי יִמְצָא; וְרָחֹק מִפְּנִינִים מִכְרָהּ

'eshet-chayil mi yimtza; verachok mippeninim michrah

A woman of valour who can find? for her price is far above rubies.

בָּטַח בָּהּ, לֵב בַּעְלָהּ; וְשָׁלָל, לֹא יֶחְסָר

batach bah lev ba'lah; veshalal, lo yechsar

The heart of her husband doth safely trust in her, and he hath no lack of gain.

גְּמָלַתְהוּ טוֹב וְלֹא-רָע--כֹּל, יְמֵי חַיֶּיהָ

gemalat'hu tov velo-ra'; kol yemei chayeih

She doeth him good and not evil all the days of her life.

דָּרְשָׁה, צֶמֶר וּפִשְׁתִּים; וַתַּעַשׂ, בְּחֵפֶץ כַּפֶּיהָ

dareshah tzemer ufishtim; vatta'as, bechefetz kappeiha

She seeketh wool and flax, and worketh willingly with her hands.

הָיְתָה, כָּאֳנִיּוֹת סוֹחֵר; מִמֶּרְחָק, תָּבִיא לַחְמָהּ

hayetah ko'oniyot socher; mimmerchak, tavi lachmah

She is like the merchant-ships; she bringeth her food from afar.

וַתָּקָם, בְּעוֹד לַיְלָה--וַתִּתֵּן טֶרֶף לְבֵיתָהּ; וְחֹק, לְנַעֲרֹתֶיהָ

vattakom be'od laylah, vattitten teref leveitah; vechok, lena'aroteiha

She riseth also while it is yet night, and giveth food to her household, and a portion to her maidens.

זָמְמָה שָׂדֶה, וַתִּקָּחֵהוּ; מִפְּרִי כַפֶּיהָ, נָטְעָה כָּרֶם

zamemah sadeh vattikkachehu; mipperi chappeiha, nate'ah karem

She considereth a field, and buyeth it; with the fruit of her hands she planteth a vineyard.

חָגְרָה בְעוֹז מָתְנֶיהָ; וַתְּאַמֵּץ, זְרוֹעֹתֶיהָ

chagerah ve'oz moteneiha; vatte'ammetz, zero'oteiha

She girdeth her loins with strength, and maketh strong her arms.

טָעֲמָה, כִּי-טוֹב סַחְרָהּ; לֹא-יִכְבֶּה בַלַּיְלָה נֵרָהּ

ta'amah ki-tov sachrah; lo-yichbeh vallaylah nerah

She perceiveth that her merchandise is good; her lamp goeth not out by night.

יָדֶיהָ, שִׁלְּחָה בַכִּישׁוֹר; וְכַפֶּיהָ, תָּמְכוּ פָלֶךְ

yadeiha shillechah vakkishor; vechappeiha, tamechu falech

She layeth her hands to the distaff, and her hands hold the spindle.

זַרְזִיר מָתְנַיִם אוֹ-תָיִשׁ; וּמֶלֶךְ, אַלְקוּם עִמּוֹ
zarzir motenayim o-tayish; umelech, alkum immo
The greyhound; the he-goat also; and the king, against whom there is no rising up.

אִם-נָבַלְתָּ בְהִתְנַשֵּׂא; וְאִם-זַמּוֹתָ, יָד לְפֶה
'im-navalta vehitnasse; ve'im-zammota, yad lefeh
If thou hast done foolishly in lifting up thyself, or if thou hast planned devices, lay thy hand upon thy mouth.

כִּי מִיץ חָלָב, יוֹצִיא חֶמְאָה--וּמִיץ-אַף, יוֹצִיא דָם
ki mitz chalav yotzi chem'ah, umitz-'af yotzi dam
For the churning of milk bringeth forth curd, and the wringing of the nose bringeth forth blood;

וּמִיץ אַפַּיִם, יוֹצִיא רִיב
umitz appayim, yotzi riv
so the forcing of wrath bringeth forth strife.

לא

דִּבְרֵי, לְמוֹאֵל מֶלֶךְ--מַשָּׂא, אֲשֶׁר-יִסְּרַתּוּ אִמּוֹ
Divrei lemu'el melech; massa, asher-yisserattu immo
The words of king Lemuel; the burden wherewith his mother corrected him.

מַה-בְּרִי, וּמַה-בַּר-בִּטְנִי; וּמֶה, בַּר-נְדָרָי
mah-beri umah-bar-bitni; umeh bar-nedarai
What, my son? and what, O son of my womb? and what, O son of my vows?

אַל-תִּתֵּן לַנָּשִׁים חֵילֶךָ; וּדְרָכֶיךָ, לַמְחוֹת מְלָכִין
'al-titten lannashim cheilecha; uderacheicha, lamchot melachin
Give not thy strength unto women, nor thy ways to that which destroyeth kings.

אַל לַמְלָכִים, לְמוֹאֵל--אַל לַמְלָכִים שְׁתוֹ-יָיִן; וּלְרוֹזְנִים, אֵי שֵׁכָר
'al lamlachim lemo'el, al lamlachim sheto-yayin; ulerozenim, ei shechar
It is not for kings, O Lemuel, it is not for kings to drink wine: nor for princes to say: 'Where is strong drink?'

פֶּן-יִשְׁתֶּה, וְיִשְׁכַּח מְחֻקָּק; וִישַׁנֶּה, דִּין כָּל-בְּנֵי-עֹנִי
pen-yishteh veyishkach mechukkak; vishanneh din kol-benei-'oni
Lest they drink, and forget that which is decreed, and pervert the justice due to any that is afflicted.

תְּנוּ-שֵׁכָר לְאוֹבֵד; וְיַיִן, לְמָרֵי נָפֶשׁ
tenu-shechar le'oved; veyayin lemarei nafesh
Give strong drink unto him that is ready to perish, and wine unto the bitter in soul;

יִשְׁתֶּה, וְיִשְׁכַּח רִישׁוֹ; וַעֲמָלוֹ, לֹא יִזְכָּר-עוֹד
yishteh veyishkach risho; va'amalo, lo yizkor-'od
Let him drink, and forget his poverty, and remember his misery no more

דֶּרֶךְ-אֳנִיָּה בְלֶב-יָם--וְדֶרֶךְ גֶּבֶר בְּעַלְמָה

derech-'oniyah velev-yam; vederech gever be'almah

the way of a ship in the midst of the sea; and the way of a man with a young woman.

כֵּן, דֶּרֶךְ אִשָּׁה--מְנָאָפֶת: אָכְלָה, וּמָחֲתָה פִיהָ; וְאָמְרָה, לֹא-פָעַלְתִּי אָוֶן

ken derech ishah, mena'afet achelah umachatah fiha; ve'amerah, lo-fa'alti aven

So is the way of an adulterous woman; she eateth, and wipeth her mouth, and saith: 'I have done no wickedness.'

תַּחַת שָׁלוֹשׁ, רָגְזָה אֶרֶץ; וְתַחַת אַרְבַּע, לֹא-תוּכַל שְׂאֵת

tachat shalosh ragezah eretz; vetachat arba', lo-tuchal se'et

For three things the earth doth quake, and for four it cannot endure:

תַּחַת-עֶבֶד, כִּי יִמְלוֹךְ; וְנָבָל, כִּי יִשְׂבַּע-לָחֶם

tachat-'eved ki yimloch; venaval, ki yisba'-lachem

For a servant when he reigneth; and a churl when he is filled with food;

תַּחַת שְׂנוּאָה, כִּי תִבָּעֵל; וְשִׁפְחָה, כִּי-תִירַשׁ גְּבִרְתָּהּ

tachat senu'ah ki tibba'el; veshifchah, ki-tirash gevirtah

For an odious woman when she is married; and a handmaid that is heir to her mistress.

אַרְבָּעָה הֵם, קְטַנֵּי-אָרֶץ; וְהֵמָּה, חֲכָמִים מְחֻכָּמִים

'arba'ah hem ketannei-'aretz; vehemmah, chachamim mechukkamim

There are four things which are little upon the earth, but they are exceeding wise:

הַנְּמָלִים, עַם לֹא-עָז; וַיָּכִינוּ בַקַּיִץ לַחְמָם

hannemalim am lo-'az; vayachinu vakkayitz lachmam

The ants are a people not strong, yet they provide their food in the summer;

שְׁפַנִּים, עַם לֹא-עָצוּם; וַיָּשִׂימוּ בַסֶּלַע בֵּיתָם

shefannim am lo-'atzum; vayasimu vassela beitam

The rock-badgers are but a feeble folk, yet make they their houses in the crags;

מֶלֶךְ, אֵין לָאַרְבֶּה; וַיֵּצֵא חֹצֵץ כֻּלּוֹ

melech ein la'arbeh; vayetzei chotzetz kullo

The locusts have no king, yet go they forth all of them by bands;

שְׂמָמִית, בְּיָדַיִם תְּתַפֵּשׂ; וְהִיא, בְּהֵיכְלֵי מֶלֶךְ

semamit beyadayim tetappes; vehi, beheichelei melech

The spider thou canst take with the hands, yet is she in kings' palaces.

שְׁלֹשָׁה הֵמָּה, מֵיטִיבֵי צָעַד; וְאַרְבָּעָה, מֵיטִבֵי לָכֶת

sheloshah hemmah meitivei tza'ad; ve'arba'ah, meitivei lachet

There are three things which are stately in their march, yea, four which are stately in going:

.לַיִשׁ, גִּבּוֹר בַּבְּהֵמָה; וְלֹא-יָשׁוּב, מִפְּנֵי-כֹל

layish gibbor babbehemah; velo-yashuv, mippenei-chol

The lion, which is mightiest among beasts, and turneth not away for any;

דּוֹר, אָבִיו יְקַלֵּל; וְאֶת-אִמּוֹ, לֹא יְבָרֵךְ

dor aviv yekallel; ve'et-'immo, lo yevarech

There is a generation that curse their father, and do not bless their mother.

דּוֹר, טָהוֹר בְּעֵינָיו; וּמִצֹּאָתוֹ, לֹא רֻחָץ

dor tahor be'einav; umitzo'ato, lo ruchatz

There is a generation that are pure in their own eyes, and yet are not washed from their filthiness.

דּוֹר, מָה-רָמוּ עֵינָיו; וְעַפְעַפָּיו, יִנָּשֵׂאוּ

dor mah-ramu einav; ve'af'appav, yinnase'u

There is a generation, Oh how lofty are their eyes! and their eyelids are lifted up.

דּוֹר, חֲרָבוֹת שִׁנָּיו--וּמַאֲכָלוֹת מְתַלְּעֹתָיו

dor charavot shinnav uma'achalot metalle'otav

There is a generation whose teeth are as swords, and their great teeth as knives,

לֶאֱכֹל עֲנִיִּים מֵאֶרֶץ; וְאֶבְיוֹנִים, מֵאָדָם

le'echol aniyim me'eretz; ve'evyonim, me'adam

to devour the poor from off the earth, and the needy from among men.

לַעֲלוּקָה, שְׁתֵּי בָנוֹת--הַב הַב

la'alukah shetei vanot hav hav

The horseleech hath two daughters: 'Give, give.'

שָׁלוֹשׁ הֵנָּה, לֹא תִשְׂבַּעְנָה; אַרְבַּע, לֹא-אָמְרוּ הוֹן

shalosh hennah lo tisba'nah; arba', lo-'ameru hon

There are three things that are never satisfied, yea, four that say not: 'Enough':

שְׁאוֹל, וְעֹצֶר-רָחַם: אֶרֶץ, לֹא-שָׂבְעָה מַיִם; וְאֵשׁ, לֹא-אָמְרָה הוֹן

she'ol ve'otzer racham eretz lo-save'ah mayim; ve'esh, lo-'amerah hon

The grave; and the barren womb; the earth that is not satisfied with water; and the fire that saith not: 'Enough.'

עַיִן, תִּלְעַג לְאָב--וְתָבֻז לִיקְּהַת-אֵם

'ayin til'ag le'av vetavuz likkahat-'em

The eye that mocketh at his father, and despiseth to obey his mother,

יִקְּרוּהָ, עֹרְבֵי-נַחַל; וְיֹאכְלוּהָ בְנֵי-נָשֶׁר

yikkeruha orevei-nachal; veyocheluha venei-nasher

the ravens of the valley shall pick it out, and the young vultures shall eat it.

שְׁלֹשָׁה הֵמָּה, נִפְלְאוּ מִמֶּנִּי; וְאַרְבָּעָה, לֹא יְדַעְתִּים

sheloshah hemmah nifle'u mimmenni; ve'arba'ah, lo yeda'tim

There are three things which are too wonderful for me, yea, four which I know not:

דֶּרֶךְ הַנֶּשֶׁר, בַּשָּׁמַיִם--דֶּרֶךְ נָחָשׁ, עֲלֵי-צוּר

derech hannesher bashamayim derech nachash, alei tzur

The way of an eagle in the air; the way of a serpent upon a rock;

כִּי בַעַר אָנֹכִי מֵאִישׁ; וְלֹא-בִינַת אָדָם לִי

ki va'ar anochi me'ish; velo-vinat adam li

Surely I am brutish, unlike a man, and have not the understanding of a man;

וְלֹא-לָמַדְתִּי חָכְמָה; וְדַעַת קְדֹשִׁים אֵדָע.

velo-lamadti chochmah veda'at kedoshim eda

And I have not learned wisdom, that I should have the knowledge of the Holy One.

מִי עָלָה-שָׁמַיִם וַיֵּרַד, מִי אָסַף-רוּחַ בְּחָפְנָיו

mi alah-shamayim vayerad mi asaf-ruach bechofnav

Who hath ascended up into heaven, and descended? Who hath gathered the wind in his fists?

מִי צָרַר-מַיִם בַּשִּׂמְלָה--מִי, הֵקִים כָּל-אַפְסֵי-אָרֶץ

mi tzarar-mayim bassimlah, mi hekim kol-'afsei-'aretz

Who hath bound the waters in his garment? Who hath established all the ends of the earth?

מַה-שְּׁמוֹ וּמַה-שֶּׁם-בְּנוֹ, כִּי תֵדָע

mah-shemo umah-shem-beno, ki teda

What is his name, and what is his son's name, if thou knowest?

כָּל-אִמְרַת אֱלוֹהַּ צְרוּפָה; מָגֵן הוּא, לַחֹסִים בּוֹ

kol-'imrat eloah tzerufah; magen hu, lachosim bo

Every word of God is tried; He is a shield unto them that take refuge in Him.

אַל-תּוֹסְףְּ עַל-דְּבָרָיו: פֶּן-יוֹכִיחַ בְּךָ וְנִכְזָבְתָּ

'al-tosef al-devarav; pen-yochiach becha venichzaveta

Add thou not unto His words, lest He reprove thee, and thou be found a liar.

שְׁתַּיִם, שָׁאַלְתִּי מֵאִתָּךְ; אַל-תִּמְנַע מִמֶּנִּי, בְּטֶרֶם אָמוּת

shetayim sha'alti me'ittach; al-timna mimmenni, beterem amut

Two things have I asked of Thee; deny me them not before I die:

שָׁוְא וּדְבַר-כָּזָב, הַרְחֵק מִמֶּנִּי--רֵאשׁ וָעֹשֶׁר אַל-תִּתֶּן-לִי; הַטְרִיפֵנִי, לֶחֶם חֻקִּי.

shav udevar-kazav harchek mimmenni, resh va'osher al-titten-li; hatrifeni, lechem chukki

Remove far from me falsehood and lies; give me neither poverty nor riches; feed me with mine allotted bread;

פֶּן אֶשְׂבַּע, וְכִחַשְׁתִּי--וְאָמַרְתִּי, מִי יְהוָה

pen esba vechichashti ve'amarti, mi hashem

Lest I be full, and deny, and say: 'Who is the LORD?'

וּפֶן-אִוָּרֵשׁ וְגָנַבְתִּי; וְתָפַשְׂתִּי, שֵׁם אֱלֹהָי

ufen-'ivvaresh veganavti; vetafasti, shem elohai

Or lest I be poor, and steal, and profane the name of my God.

אַל-תַּלְשֵׁן עֶבֶד, אֶל-אֲדֹנָו: פֶּן-יְקַלֶּלְךָ וְאָשָׁמְתָּ.

'al-talshen eved el-'adonav; pen-yekallelcha ve'ashameta

Slander not a servant unto his master, lest he curse thee, and thou be found guilty.

בְּאֵין חָזוֹן, יִפָּרַע עָם; וְשֹׁמֵר תּוֹרָה אַשְׁרֵהוּ

be'ein chazon yippara am; veshomer torah ashrehu

Where there is no vision, the people cast off restraint; but he that keepeth the law, happy is he.

בִּדְבָרִים, לֹא-יִוָּסֶר עָבֶד: כִּי-יָבִין, וְאֵין מַעֲנֶה

bidvarim lo-yivvaser aved; ki-yavin, ve'ein ma'aneh

A servant will not be corrected by words; for though he understand, there will be no response.

חָזִיתָ--אִישׁ, אָץ בִּדְבָרָיו: תִּקְוָה לִכְסִיל מִמֶּנּוּ

chazita, ish atz bidvarav; tikvah lichsil mimmennu

Seest thou a man that is hasty in his words? there is more hope for a fool than for him.

מְפַנֵּק מִנֹּעַר עַבְדּוֹ; וְאַחֲרִיתוֹ, יִהְיֶה מָנוֹן

mefannek minno'ar avdo; ve'acharito, yihyeh manon

He that delicately bringeth up his servant from a child shall have him become master at the last.

אִישׁ-אַף, יְגָרֶה מָדוֹן; וּבַעַל חֵמָה רַב-פָּשַׁע

'ish-'af yegareh madon; uva'al chemah rav-pasha

An angry man stirreth up strife, and a wrathful man aboundeth in transgression.

גַּאֲוַת אָדָם, תַּשְׁפִּילֶנּוּ; וּשְׁפַל-רוּחַ, יִתְמֹךְ כָּבוֹד

ga'avat adom tashpilennu; ushefal-ruach, yitmoch kavod

A man's pride shall bring him low; but he that is of a lowly spirit shall attain to honour.

חוֹלֵק עִם-גַּנָּב, שׂוֹנֵא נַפְשׁוֹ; אָלָה יִשְׁמַע, וְלֹא יַגִּיד

cholek im-gannav sonei nafsho; alah yishma', velo yaggid

Whoso is partner with a thief hateth his own soul: he heareth the adjuration and uttereth nothing.

חֶרְדַּת אָדָם, יִתֵּן מוֹקֵשׁ; וּבוֹטֵחַ בַּיהוָה יְשֻׂגָּב

cherdat adom yitten mokesh; uvoteach bahashem yesuggav

The fear of man bringeth a snare; but whoso putteth his trust in the LORD shall be set up on high.

רַבִּים, מְבַקְשִׁים פְּנֵי-מוֹשֵׁל; וּמֵיְהוָה, מִשְׁפַּט-אִישׁ

rabbim mevakshim penei-moshel; umehashem, mishpat-'ish

Many seek the ruler's favour; but a man's judgment cometh from the LORD.

תּוֹעֲבַת צַדִּיקִים, אִישׁ עָוֶל; וְתוֹעֲבַת רָשָׁע יְשַׁר-דָּרֶךְ

to'avat tzaddikim ish avel; veto'avat rasha yeshar-darech

An unjust man is an abomination to the righteous; and he that is upright in the way is an abomination to the wicked.

ל

דִּבְרֵי, אָגוּר בִּן-יָקֶה--הַמַּשָּׂא: נְאֻם הַגֶּבֶר, לְאִיתִיאֵל; לְאִיתִיאֵל וְאֻכָל

Divrei agur bin-yakeh, hammassa ne'um haggever le'iti'el; le'iti'el ve'uchal

The words of Agur the son of Jakeh; the burden. The man saith unto Ithiel, unto Ithiel and Ucal:

בְּפֶשַׁע אִישׁ רָע מוֹקֵשׁ; וְצַדִּיק, יָרוּן וְשָׂמֵחַ
befesha ish ra mokesh; vetzaddik, yarun vesameach
In the transgression of an evil man there is a snare; but the righteous doth sing and rejoice.

יֹדֵעַ צַדִּיק, דִּין דַּלִּים; רָשָׁע, לֹא-יָבִין דָּעַת
yodea tzaddik din dallim; rasha', lo-yavin da'at
The righteous taketh knowledge of the cause of the poor; the wicked understandeth not knowledge.

אַנְשֵׁי לָצוֹן, יָפִיחוּ קִרְיָה; וַחֲכָמִים, יָשִׁיבוּ אָף
'anshei latzon yafichu kiryah; vachachamim, yashivu af
Scornful men set a city in a blaze; but wise men turn away wrath.

אִישׁ-חָכָם--נִשְׁפָּט, אֶת-אִישׁ אֱוִיל: וְרָגַז וְשָׂחַק, וְאֵין נָחַת
'ish-chacham, nishpot et-'ish evil; veragaz vesachak, ve'ein nachat
If a wise man contendeth with a foolish man, whether he be angry or laugh, there will be no rest.

אַנְשֵׁי דָמִים, יִשְׂנְאוּ-תָם; וִישָׁרִים, יְבַקְשׁוּ נַפְשׁוֹ
'anshei damim yisne'u-tam; viysharim, yevakshu nafsho
The men of blood hate him that is sincere; and as for the upright, they seek his life.

כָּל-רוּחוֹ, יוֹצִיא כְסִיל; וְחָכָם, בְּאָחוֹר יְשַׁבְּחֶנָּה
kol-rucho yotzi chesil; vechacham, be'achor yeshabbechennah
A fool spendeth all his spirit; but a wise man stilleth it within him.

מֹשֵׁל, מַקְשִׁיב עַל-דְּבַר-שָׁקֶר--כָּל-מְשָׁרְתָיו רְשָׁעִים
moshel makshiv al-devar-shaker; kol-mesharetav resha'im
If a ruler hearkeneth to falsehood, all his servants are wicked.

רָשׁ וְאִישׁ תְּכָכִים נִפְגָּשׁוּ--מֵאִיר עֵינֵי שְׁנֵיהֶם יְהוָה
rash ve'ish techachim nifgashu; me'ir-'einei sheneihem hashem
The poor man and the oppressor meet together; the LORD giveth light to the eyes of them both.

מֶלֶךְ שׁוֹפֵט בֶּאֱמֶת דַּלִּים--כִּסְאוֹ, לָעַד יִכּוֹן
melech shofet be'emet dallim; kis'o, la'ad yikkon
The king that faithfully judgeth the poor, his throne shall be established for ever.

שֵׁבֶט וְתוֹכַחַת, יִתֵּן חָכְמָה; וְנַעַר מְשֻׁלָּח, מֵבִישׁ אִמּוֹ
shevet vetochachat yitten chochmah vena'ar meshullach, mevish immo
The rod and reproof give wisdom; but a child left to himself causeth shame to his mother.

בִּרְבוֹת רְשָׁעִים, יִרְבֶּה-פָּשַׁע; וְצַדִּיקִים, בְּמַפַּלְתָּם יִרְאוּ
birvot resha'im yirbeh-pasha'; vetzaddikim, bemappaltam yir'u
When the wicked are increased, transgression increaseth; but the righteous shall gaze upon their fall.

יַסֵּר בִּנְךָ, וִינִיחֶךָ; וְיִתֵּן מַעֲדַנִּים לְנַפְשֶׁךָ
yasser bincha viynichecha; veyitten ma'adannim lenafshecha
Correct thy son, and he will give thee rest; yea, he will give delight unto thy soul.

גּוֹזֵל, אָבִיו וְאִמּוֹ--וְאֹמֵר

gozel aviv ve'immo, ve'omer

Whoso robbeth his father or his mother, and saith:

אֵין-פָּשַׁע: חָבֵר הוּא, לְאִישׁ מַשְׁחִית

ein-pasha'; chaver hu, le'ish mashchit

'It is no transgression', the same is the companion of a destroyer.

רְחַב-נֶפֶשׁ, יְגָרֶה מָדוֹן; וּבֹטֵחַ עַל-יְהוָה יְדֻשָּׁן

rechav-nefesh yegareh madon; uvoteach al-hashem yedushan

He that is of a greedy spirit stirreth up strife; but he that putteth his trust in the LORD shall be abundantly gratified.

בּוֹטֵחַ בְּלִבּוֹ, הוּא כְסִיל; וְהוֹלֵךְ בְּחָכְמָה, הוּא יִמָּלֵט

boteach belibbo hu chesil; veholech bechochmah hu yimmalet

He that trusteth in his own heart is a fool; but whoso walketh wisely, he shall escape.

נוֹתֵן לָרָשׁ, אֵין מַחְסוֹר; וּמַעְלִים עֵינָיו, רַב-מְאֵרוֹת

noten larash ein machsor; uma'lim einav, rav-me'erot

He that giveth unto the poor shall not lack; but he that hideth his eyes shall have many a curse.

בְּקוּם רְשָׁעִים, יִסָּתֵר אָדָם; וּבְאָבְדָם, יִרְבּוּ צַדִּיקִים

bekum resha'im yissater adam; uve'avedam, yirbu tzaddikim

When the wicked rise, men hide themselves; but when they perish, the righteous increase.

כט

אִישׁ תּוֹכָחוֹת, מַקְשֶׁה-עֹרֶף--פֶּתַע יִשָּׁבֵר, וְאֵין מַרְפֵּא

Ish tochachot maksheh-'oref; peta yishaver, ve'ein marpe

He that being often reproved hardeneth his neck shall suddenly be broken, and that without remedy.

בִּרְבוֹת צַדִּיקִים, יִשְׂמַח הָעָם; וּבִמְשֹׁל רָשָׁע, יֵאָנַח עָם

birvot tzaddikim yismach ha'am; uvimshol rasha', ye'anach am

When the righteous are increased, the people rejoice; but when the wicked beareth rule, the people sigh.

אִישׁ-אֹהֵב חָכְמָה, יְשַׂמַּח אָבִיו; וְרֹעֶה זוֹנוֹת, יְאַבֶּד-הוֹן

'ish-'ohev chochmah yesammach aviv; vero'eh zonot, ye'abbed-hon

Whoso loveth wisdom rejoiceth his father; but he that keepeth company with harlots wasteth his substance.

מֶלֶךְ--בְּמִשְׁפָּט, יַעֲמִיד אָרֶץ; וְאִישׁ תְּרוּמוֹת יֶהֶרְסֶנָּה

melech, bemishpot ya'amid aretz; ve'ish terumot yehersennah

The king by justice establisheth the land; but he that exacteth gifts overthroweth it.

גֶּבֶר, מַחֲלִיק עַל-רֵעֵהוּ; רֶשֶׁת, פּוֹרֵשׂ עַל-פְּעָמָיו

gever machalik al-re'ehu; reshet, pores al-pe'amav

A man that flattereth his neighbour spreadeth a net for his steps.

אַשְׁרֵי אָדָם, מְפַחֵד תָּמִיד; וּמַקְשֶׁה לִבּוֹ, יִפּוֹל בְּרָעָה

'ashrei adam mefached tamid; umaksheh libbo, yippol bera'ah

Happy is the man that feareth alway; but he that hardeneth his heart shall fall into evil.

אֲרִי-נֹהֵם, וְדֹב שׁוֹקֵק--מֹשֵׁל רָשָׁע, עַל עַם-דָּל

'ari-nohem vedov shokek; moshel rasha', al am-dal

As a roaring lion, and a ravenous bear; so is a wicked ruler over a poor people.

נָגִיד--חֲסַר תְּבוּנוֹת, וְרַב מַעֲשַׁקּוֹת

nagid, chasar tevunot verav ma'ashakkot

The prince that lacketh understanding is also a great oppressor;

שֹׂנֵא בֶצַע, יַאֲרִיךְ יָמִים

sonei vetza', ya'arich yamim

but he that hateth covetousness shall prolong his days.

אָדָם, עָשֻׁק בְּדַם-נָפֶשׁ--עַד-בּוֹר יָנוּס, אַל-יִתְמְכוּ-בוֹ

'adom ashuk bedam-nafesh; ad-bor yanus, al-yitmechu-vo

A man that is laden with the blood of any person shall hasten his steps unto the pit; none will support him.

הוֹלֵךְ תָּמִים, יִוָּשֵׁעַ; וְנֶעְקַשׁ דְּרָכַיִם, יִפּוֹל בְּאֶחָת

holech tamim yivvashea'; vene'kash derachayim, yippol be'echat

Whoso walketh uprightly shall be saved; but he that is perverse in his ways shall fall at once.

עֹבֵד אַדְמָתוֹ, יִשְׂבַּע-לָחֶם

'oved admato yisba'-lachem

He that tilleth his ground shall have plenty of bread;

וּמְרַדֵּף רֵיקִים, יִשְׂבַּע-רִישׁ

umeraddef rekim, yisba'-rish

but he that followeth after vain things shall have poverty enough.

אִישׁ אֱמוּנוֹת, רַב-בְּרָכוֹת; וְאָץ לְהַעֲשִׁיר, לֹא יִנָּקֶה

'ish emunot rav-berachot; ve'atz leha'ashir, lo yinnakeh

A faithful man shall abound with blessings; but he that maketh haste to be rich shall not be unpunished.

הַכֵּר-פָּנִים לֹא-טוֹב; וְעַל-פַּת-לֶחֶם, יִפְשַׁע-גָּבֶר

hakker-panim lo-tov; ve'al-pat-lechem, yifsha'-gaver

To have respect of persons is not good; for a man will transgress for a piece of bread.

נִבְהָל לַהוֹן--אִישׁ, רַע עָיִן; וְלֹא-יֵדַע, כִּי-חֶסֶר יְבֹאֶנּוּ

nivhal lahon, ish ra ayin; velo-yeda ki-cheser yevo'ennu

He that hath an evil eye hasteneth after riches, and knoweth not that want shall come upon him.

מוֹכִיחַ אָדָם אַחֲרַי, חֵן יִמְצָא--מִמַּחֲלִיק לָשׁוֹן

mochiach adam acharai chen yimtza; mimmachalik lashon

He that rebuketh a man shall in the end find more favour than he that flattereth with the tongue.

גֶּבֶר-רָשׁ, וְעֹשֵׁק דַּלִּים--מָטָר סֹחֵף, וְאֵין לָחֶם

gever rash ve'oshek dallim; matar sochef, ve'ein lachem

A poor man that oppresseth the weak is like a sweeping rain which leaveth no food.

עֹזְבֵי תוֹרָה, יְהַלְלוּ רָשָׁע; וְשֹׁמְרֵי תוֹרָה, יִתְגָּרוּ בָם

'ozevei torah yehalelu rasha'; veshomerei torah, yitgaru vam

They that forsake the law praise the wicked; but such as keep the law contend with them.

אַנְשֵׁי-רָע, לֹא-יָבִינוּ מִשְׁפָּט; וּמְבַקְשֵׁי יְהוָה, יָבִינוּ כֹל

'anshei-ra lo-yavinu mishpat; umevakshei hashem yavinu chol

Evil men understand not justice; but they that seek the LORD understand all things.

טוֹב-רָשׁ, הוֹלֵךְ בְּתֻמּוֹ--מֵעִקֵּשׁ דְּרָכַיִם, וְהוּא עָשִׁיר

tov-rash holech betummo; me'ikkesh derachayim, vehu ashir

Better is the poor that walketh in his integrity, than he that is perverse in his ways, though he be rich.

נוֹצֵר תּוֹרָה, בֵּן מֵבִין; וְרֹעֶה זוֹלְלִים, יַכְלִים אָבִיו

notzer torah ben mevin; vero'eh zolelim, yachlim aviv

A wise son observeth the teaching; but he that is a companion of gluttonous men shameth his father.

מַרְבֶּה הוֹנוֹ, בְּנֶשֶׁךְ וְתַרְבִּית--לְחוֹנֵן דַּלִּים יִקְבְּצֶנּוּ

marbeh hono beneshech vetarbit; lechonen dallim yikbetzennu

He that augmenteth his substance by interest and increase, gathereth it for him that is gracious to the poor.

מֵסִיר אָזְנוֹ, מִשְּׁמֹעַ תּוֹרָה--גַּם תְּפִלָּתוֹ, תּוֹעֵבָה

mesir ozeno mishemoa torah; gam-tefillato, to'evah

He that turneth away his ear from hearing the law, even his prayer is an abomination.

מַשְׁגֶּה יְשָׁרִים, בְּדֶרֶךְ רָע

mashgeh yesharim bederech ra'

Whoso causeth the upright to go astray in an evil way,

בִּשְׁחוּתוֹ הוּא-יִפּוֹל; וּתְמִימִים, יִנְחֲלוּ-טוֹב

bishchuto hu-yippol; utemimim, yinchalu-tov

he shall fall himself into his own pit; but the whole-hearted shall inherit good.

חָכָם בְּעֵינָיו, אִישׁ עָשִׁיר; וְדַל מֵבִין יַחְקְרֶנּוּ

chacham be'einav ish ashir; vedal mevin yachkerennu

The rich man is wise in his own eyes; but the poor that hath understanding searcheth him through.

בַּעֲלֹץ צַדִּיקִים, רַבָּה תִפְאָרֶת; וּבְקוּם רְשָׁעִים, יְחֻפַּשׂ אָדָם

ba'alotz tzaddikim rabbah tif'aret; uvekum resha'im, yechuppas adam

When the righteous exult, there is great glory; but when the wicked rise, men must be sought for.

מְכַסֶּה פְשָׁעָיו, לֹא יַצְלִיחַ; וּמוֹדֶה וְעֹזֵב יְרֻחָם

mechasseh fesha'av lo yatzliach; umodeh ve'ozev yerucham

He that covereth his transgressions shall not prosper; but whoso confesseth and forsaketh them shall obtain mercy.

שְׁאוֹל וַאֲבַדֹּה, לֹא תִשְׂבַּעְנָה; וְעֵינֵי הָאָדָם, לֹא תִשְׂבַּעְנָה
she'ol va'avaddo lo tisba'nah; ve'einei ha'adam, lo tisba'nah
The nether-world and Destruction are never satiated; so the eyes of man are never satiated.

מַצְרֵף לַכֶּסֶף, וְכוּר לַזָּהָב; וְאִישׁ, לְפִי מַהֲלָלוֹ
matzref lakkesef vechur lazzahav; ve'ish, lefi mahalalo
The refining pot is for silver, and the furnace for gold, and a man is tried by his praise.

אִם תִּכְתּוֹשׁ-אֶת-הָאֱוִיל, בַּמַּכְתֵּשׁ בְּתוֹךְ הָרִיפוֹת--בַּעֱלִי: לֹא-תָסוּר מֵעָלָיו, אִוַּלְתּוֹ
'im tichtosh-'et-ha'evil bammachtesh betoch harifot ba'eli; lo-tasur me'alav, ivvalto
Though thou shouldest bray a fool in a mortar with a pestle among groats, yet will not his foolishness depart from him.

יָדֹעַ תֵּדַע, פְּנֵי צֹאנֶךָ; שִׁית לִבְּךָ, לַעֲדָרִים
yadoa teda penei tzonecha; shit libbecha, la'adarim
Be thou diligent to know the state of thy flocks, and look well to thy herds;

כִּי לֹא לְעוֹלָם חֹסֶן; וְאִם-נֵזֶר, לְדוֹר וָדוֹר
ki lo le'olam chosen; ve'im-nezer, ledor vador
For riches are not for ever; and doth the crown endure unto all generations?

גָּלָה חָצִיר, וְנִרְאָה-דֶשֶׁא; וְנֶאֶסְפוּ, עִשְּׂבוֹת הָרִים
galah chatzir venir'ah-deshe; vene'esfu, issevot harim
When the hay is mown, and the tender grass showeth itself, and the herbs of the mountains are gathered in;

כְּבָשִׂים לִלְבוּשֶׁךָ; וּמְחִיר שָׂדֶה, עַתּוּדִים
kevasim lilvushecha; umechir sadeh, attudim
The lambs will be for thy clothing, and the goats the price for a field.

וְדֵי, חֲלֵב עִזִּים--לְלַחְמְךָ, לְלֶחֶם בֵּיתֶךָ; וְחַיִּים, לְנַעֲרוֹתֶיךָ
vedei chalev izzim, lelachmecha lelechem beitecha; vechayim, lena'aroteicha
And there will be goats' milk enough for thy food, for the food of thy household; and maintenance for thy maidens.

כח

נָסוּ וְאֵין-רֹדֵף רָשָׁע; וְצַדִּיקִים, כִּכְפִיר יִבְטָח
Nasu ve'ein-rodef rasha'; vetzaddikim, kichfir yivtach
The wicked flee when no man pursueth; but the righteous are secure as a young lion.

בְּפֶשַׁע אֶרֶץ, רַבִּים שָׂרֶיהָ
befesha eretz rabbim sareiha
For the transgression of a land many are the princes thereof;

וּבְאָדָם מֵבִין יֹדֵעַ, כֵּן יַאֲרִיךְ
uve'adam mevin yodea', ken ya'arich
but by a man of understanding and knowledge established order shall long continue.

שֶׁמֶן וּקְטֹרֶת, יְשַׂמַּח-לֵב; וּמֶתֶק רֵעֵהוּ, מֵעֲצַת-נָפֶשׁ

shemen uketoret yesammach-lev; umetek re'ehu, me'atzat-nafesh

Ointment and perfume rejoice the heart; so doth the sweetness of a man's friend by hearty counsel.

רֵעֲךָ וְרֵעַ אָבִיךָ, אַל-תַּעֲזֹב, וּבֵית אָחִיךָ, אַל-תָּבוֹא בְּיוֹם אֵידֶךָ

re'acha verea avicha al-ta'azov, uveit achicha, al-tavo beyom eidecha

Thine own friend, and thy father's friend, forsake not; neither go into thy brother's house in the day of thy calamity;

טוֹב שָׁכֵן קָרוֹב, מֵאָח רָחוֹק

tov shachen karov, me'ach rachok

better is a neighbour that is near than a brother far off.

חֲכַם בְּנִי, וְשַׂמַּח לִבִּי; וְאָשִׁיבָה חֹרְפִי דָבָר

chacham beni vesammach libbi; ve'ashivah chorefi davar

My son, be wise, and make my heart glad, that I may answer him that taunteth me.

עָרוּם, רָאָה רָעָה נִסְתָּר; פְּתָאיִם, עָבְרוּ נֶעֱנָשׁוּ

'arum ra'ah ra'ah nistar; petayim, averu ne'enashu

A prudent man seeth the evil, and hideth himself; but the thoughtless pass on, and are punished.

קַח-בִּגְדוֹ, כִּי-עָרַב זָר; וּבְעַד נָכְרִיָּה חַבְלֵהוּ

kach-bigdo ki-'arav zar; uve'ad nacheriyah chavlehu

Take his garment that is surety for a stranger; and hold him in pledge that is surety for an alien woman.

מְבָרֵךְ רֵעֵהוּ, בְּקוֹל גָּדוֹל--בַּבֹּקֶר הַשְׁכֵּים: קְלָלָה, תֵּחָשֶׁב לוֹ

mevarech re'ehu bekol gadol babboker hashkeim; kelalah, techashev lo

He that blesseth his friend with a loud voice, rising early in the morning, it shall be counted a curse to him.

דֶּלֶף טוֹרֵד, בְּיוֹם סַגְרִיר; וְאֵשֶׁת מִדְיָנִים, נִשְׁתָּוָה

delef tored beyom sagrir; ve'eshet midyanim, nishtavah

A continual dropping in a very rainy day and a contentious woman are alike;

צֹפְנֶיהָ צָפַן-רוּחַ; וְשֶׁמֶן יְמִינוֹ יִקְרָא

tzofeneiha tzafan-ruach; veshemen yemino yikra

He that would hide her hideth the wind, and the ointment of his right hand betrayeth itself.

בַּרְזֶל בְּבַרְזֶל יָחַד; וְאִישׁ, יַחַד פְּנֵי-רֵעֵהוּ

barzel bevarzel yachad; ve'ish, yachad penei-re'ehu

Iron sharpeneth iron; so a man sharpeneth the countenance of his friend.

נֹצֵר תְּאֵנָה, יֹאכַל פִּרְיָהּ; וְשֹׁמֵר אֲדֹנָיו יְכֻבָּד

notzer te'enah yochal piryah; veshomer adonav yechubbad

Whoso keepeth the fig-tree shall eat the fruit thereof; and he that waiteth on his master shall be honoured.

כַּמַּיִם, הַפָּנִים לַפָּנִים--כֵּן לֵב-הָאָדָם, לָאָדָם

kammayim happanim lappanim; ken lev-ha'adam, la'adam

As in water face answereth to face, so the heart of man to man.

תְּכַסֶּה שִׂנְאָה, בְּמַשָּׁאוֹן; תִּגָּלֶה רָעָתוֹ בְקָהָל
tikkasseh sin'ah bemasha'on; tiggaleh ra'ato vekahal
Though his hatred be concealed with deceit, his wickedness shall be revealed before the congregation.

כֹּרֶה-שַּׁחַת, בָּהּ יִפּוֹל; וְגוֹלֵל אֶבֶן, אֵלָיו תָּשׁוּב
koreh-shachat bah yippol; vegolel even elav tashuv
Whoso diggeth a pit shall fall therein; and he that rolleth a stone, it shall return upon him.

לְשׁוֹן-שֶׁקֶר, יִשְׂנָא דַכָּיו; וּפֶה חָלָק, יַעֲשֶׂה מִדְחֶה
leshon-sheker yisna dakkav; ufeh chalak, ya'aseh midcheh
A lying tongue hateth those that are crushed by it; and a flattering mouth worketh ruin.

כז

אַל-תִּתְהַלֵּל, בְּיוֹם מָחָר: כִּי לֹא-תֵדַע, מַה-יֵּלֶד יוֹם
Al-tit'hallel beyom machar; ki lo-teda', mah-yeled yom
Boast not thyself of to-morrow; for thou knowest not what a day may bring forth.

יְהַלֶּלְךָ זָר וְלֹא-פִיךָ; נָכְרִי, וְאַל-שְׂפָתֶיךָ
yehallelcha zar velo-ficha; nocheri, ve'al-sefateicha
Let another man praise thee, and not thine own mouth; a stranger, and not thine own lips.

כֹּבֶד-אֶבֶן, וְנֵטֶל הַחוֹל; וְכַעַס אֱוִיל, כָּבֵד מִשְּׁנֵיהֶם
koved-'even venetel hachol; vecha'as evil, kaved misheneihem
A stone is heavy, and the sand weighty; but a fool's vexation is heavier than they both.

אַכְזְרִיּוּת חֵמָה, וְשֶׁטֶף אָף; וּמִי יַעֲמֹד, לִפְנֵי קִנְאָה
'achzeriyut chemah veshetef af; umi ya'amod lifnei kin'ah
Wrath is cruel, and anger is overwhelming; but who is able to stand before jealousy?

טוֹבָה, תּוֹכַחַת מְגֻלָּה--מֵאַהֲבָה מְסֻתָּרֶת
tovah tochachat megullah; me'ahavah mesuttaret
Better is open rebuke than love that is hidden.

נֶאֱמָנִים, פִּצְעֵי אוֹהֵב; וְנַעְתָּרוֹת, נְשִׁיקוֹת שׂוֹנֵא
ne'emanim pitz'ei ohev; vena'tarot, neshikot sone
Faithful are the wounds of a friend; but the kisses of an enemy are importunate.

נֶפֶשׁ שְׂבֵעָה, תָּבוּס נֹפֶת; וְנֶפֶשׁ רְעֵבָה, כָּל-מַר מָתוֹק
nefesh seve'ah tavus nofet; venefesh re'evah, kol-mar matok
The full soul loatheth a honeycomb; but to the hungry soul every bitter thing is sweet.

כְּצִפּוֹר, נוֹדֶדֶת מִן-קִנָּהּ--כֵּן-אִישׁ, נוֹדֵד מִמְּקוֹמוֹ
ketzippor nodedet min-kinnah; ken-'ish, noded mimmekomo
As a bird that wandereth from her nest, so is a man that wandereth from his place.

הַדֶּלֶת, תִּסּוֹב עַל-צִירָהּ; וְעָצֵל, עַל-מִטָּתוֹ

haddelet tissov al-tzirah; ve'atzel, al-mittato

The door is turning upon its hinges, and the sluggard is still upon his bed.

טָמַן עָצֵל יָדוֹ, בַּצַּלָּחַת; נִלְאָה, לַהֲשִׁיבָהּ אֶל-פִּיו

taman atzel yado batzallachat; nil'ah, lahashivah el-piv

The sluggard burieth his hand in the dish; it wearieth him to bring it back to his mouth.

חָכָם עָצֵל בְּעֵינָיו--מִשִּׁבְעָה, מְשִׁיבֵי טָעַם

chacham atzel be'einav; mishiv'ah, meshivei ta'am

The sluggard is wiser in his own eyes than seven men that give wise answer.

מַחֲזִיק בְּאָזְנֵי-כָלֶב--עֹבֵר מִתְעַבֵּר, עַל-רִיב לֹא-לוֹ

machazik be'ozenei-chalev; over mit'abber, al-riv lo-lo

He that passeth by, and meddleth with strife not his own, is like one that taketh a dog by the ears.

כְּמִתְלַהְלֵהַּ, הַיֹּרֶה זִקִּים--חִצִּים וָמָוֶת

kemitlahleah hayoreh zikkim, chitzim vamavet

As a madman who casteth firebrands, arrows, and death;

כֵּן-אִישׁ, רִמָּה אֶת-רֵעֵהוּ; וְאָמַר, הֲלֹא-מְשַׂחֵק אָנִי

ken-'ish rimmah et-re'ehu; ve'amar, halo-mesachek ani

So is the man that deceiveth his neighbour, and saith: 'Am not I in sport?'

בְּאֶפֶס עֵצִים, תִּכְבֶּה-אֵשׁ; וּבְאֵין נִרְגָּן, יִשְׁתֹּק מָדוֹן

be'efes etzim tichbeh-'esh; uve'ein nirgan, yishtok madon

Where no wood is, the fire goeth out; and where there is no whisperer, contention ceaseth.

פֶּחָם לְגֶחָלִים, וְעֵצִים לְאֵשׁ; וְאִישׁ מִדְיָנִים, לְחַרְחַר-רִיב

pecham legechalim ve'etzim le'esh; ve'ish midyanim, lecharchar-riv

As coals are to burning coals, and wood to fire; so is a contentious man to kindle strife.

דִּבְרֵי נִרְגָּן, כְּמִתְלַהֲמִים; וְהֵם, יָרְדוּ חַדְרֵי-בָטֶן

divrei nirgan kemitlahamim; vehem, yaredu chadrei-vaten

The words of a whisperer are as dainty morsels, and they go down into the innermost parts of the body.

כֶּסֶף סִיגִים, מְצֻפֶּה עַל-חָרֶשׂ--שְׂפָתַיִם דֹּלְקִים וְלֶב-רָע

kesef sigim metzuppeh al-chares; sefatayim dolekim velev-ra

Burning lips and a wicked heart are like an earthen vessel overlaid with silver dross.

בִּשְׂפָתָו, יִנָּכֵר שׂוֹנֵא; וּבְקִרְבּוֹ, יָשִׁית מִרְמָה

bisfatav yinnacher sone; uvekirbo, yashit mirmah

He that hateth dissembleth with his lips, but he layeth up deceit within him.

כִּי-יְחַנֵּן קוֹלוֹ, אַל-תַּאֲמֶן-בּוֹ: כִּי שֶׁבַע תּוֹעֵבוֹת בְּלִבּוֹ

ki-yechannen kolo al-ta'amen-bo; ki sheva to'evot belibbo

When he speaketh fair, believe him not; for there are seven abominations in his heart.

כְּצִפּוֹר לָנוּד, כַּדְּרוֹר לָעוּף--כֵּן קִלְלַת חִנָּם, לוֹ תָבֹא
katzippor lanud kadderor la'uf; ken kilelat chinnam, lo tavo
As the wandering sparrow, as the flying swallow, so the curse that is causeless shall come home.

שׁוֹט לַסּוּס, מֶתֶג לַחֲמוֹר; וְשֵׁבֶט, לְגֵו כְּסִילִים
shot lassus meteg lachamor; veshevet, legev kesilim
A whip for the horse, a bridle for the ass, and a rod for the back of fools.

אַל-תַּעַן כְּסִיל, כְּאִוַּלְתּוֹ: פֶּן-תִּשְׁוֶה-לוֹ גַם-אָתָּה
'al-ta'an kesil ke'ivvalto; pen-tishveh-lo gam-'attah
Answer not a fool according to his folly, lest thou also be like unto him.

עֲנֵה כְסִיל, כְּאִוַּלְתּוֹ: פֶּן-יִהְיֶה חָכָם בְּעֵינָיו
'aneh chesil ke'ivvalto; pen-yihyeh chacham be'einav
Answer a fool according to his folly, lest he be wise in his own eyes.

מְקַצֶּה רַגְלַיִם, חָמָס שֹׁתֶה--שֹׁלֵחַ דְּבָרִים בְּיַד-כְּסִיל
mekatzeh raglayim chamas shoteh; sholeach devarim beyad-kesil
He that sendeth a message by the hand of a fool cutteth off his own feet, and drinketh damage.

דַּלְיוּ שֹׁקַיִם, מִפִּסֵּחַ; וּמָשָׁל, בְּפִי כְסִילִים
dalyu shokayim mippisseach; umashal, befi chesilim
The legs hang limp from the lame; so is a parable in the mouth of fools.

כִּצְרוֹר אֶבֶן, בְּמַרְגֵּמָה--כֵּן-נוֹתֵן לִכְסִיל כָּבוֹד
kitzror even bemargemah; ken-noten lichsil kavod
As a small stone in a heap of stones, so is he that giveth honour to a fool.

חוֹחַ, עָלָה בְיַד-שִׁכּוֹר; וּמָשָׁל, בְּפִי כְסִילִים
choach alah veyad-shikkor; umashal, befi chesilim
As a thorn that cometh into the hand of a drunkard, so is a parable in the mouth of fools.

רַב מְחוֹלֵל-כֹּל; וְשֹׂכֵר כְּסִיל, וְשֹׂכֵר עֹבְרִים
rav mecholel-kol vesocher kesil, vesocher overim
A master performeth all things; but he that stoppeth a fool is as one that stoppeth a flood.

כְּכֶלֶב, שָׁב עַל-קֵאוֹ--כְּסִיל, שׁוֹנֶה בְאִוַּלְתּוֹ
kechelev shav al-ke'o; kesil, shoneh ve'ivvalto
As a dog that returneth to his vomit, so is a fool that repeateth his folly.

רָאִיתָ--אִישׁ, חָכָם בְּעֵינָיו: תִּקְוָה לִכְסִיל מִמֶּנּוּ
ra'ita, ish chacham be'einav; tikvah lichsil mimmennu
Seest thou a man wise in his own eyes? there is more hope of a fool than of him.

אָמַר עָצֵל, שַׁחַל בַּדָּרֶךְ; אֲרִי, בֵּין הָרְחֹבוֹת
'amar atzel shachal baddarech; ari, bein harechovot
The sluggard saith: 'There is a lion in the way; yea, a lion is in the streets.'

שֵׁן רֹעָה, וְרֶגֶל מוּעָדֶת--מִבְטָח בּוֹגֵד, בְּיוֹם צָרָה

shen ro'ah veregel mu'adet; mivtach boged, beyom tzarah

Confidence in an unfaithful man in time of trouble is like a broken tooth, and a foot out of joint.

מַעֲדֶה-בֶּגֶד, בְּיוֹם קָרָה--חֹמֶץ עַל-נָתֶר; וְשָׁר בַּשִּׁרִים, עַל לֶב-רָע

ma'adeh beged beyom karah chometz al-nater; veshar bashirim, al lev-ra

As one that taketh off a garment in cold weather, and as vinegar upon nitre, so is he that singeth songs to a heavy heart.

אִם-רָעֵב שֹׂנַאֲךָ, הַאֲכִלֵהוּ לָחֶם; וְאִם-צָמֵא, הַשְׁקֵהוּ מָיִם

'im-ra'ev sona'acha ha'achilehu lachem; ve'im-tzame, hashkehu mayim

If thine enemy be hungry, give him bread to eat, and if he be thirsty, give him water to drink;

כִּי גֶחָלִים--אַתָּה, חֹתֶה עַל-רֹאשׁוֹ; וַיהוָה, יְשַׁלֶּם-לָךְ

ki gechalim, attah choteh al-rosho; vahashem, yeshallem-lach

For thou wilt heap coals of fire upon his head, and the LORD will reward thee.

רוּחַ צָפוֹן, תְּחוֹלֵל גָּשֶׁם; וּפָנִים נִזְעָמִים, לְשׁוֹן סָתֶר

ruach tzafon techolel gashem; ufanim niz'amim, leshon sater

The north wind bringeth forth rain, and a backbiting tongue an angry countenance.

טוֹב, שֶׁבֶת עַל-פִּנַּת-גָּג--מֵאֵשֶׁת מִדְיָנִים, וּבֵית חָבֶר

tov, shevet al-pinnat-gag; me'eshet midyanim, uveit chaver

It is better to dwell in a corner of the housetop, than in a house in common with a contentious woman.

מַיִם קָרִים, עַל-נֶפֶשׁ עֲיֵפָה; וּשְׁמוּעָה טוֹבָה, מֵאֶרֶץ מֶרְחָק

mayim karim al-nefesh ayefah; ushemu'ah tovah, me'eretz merchak

As cold waters to a faint soul, so is good news from a far country.

מַעְיָן נִרְפָּשׂ, וּמָקוֹר מָשְׁחָת--צַדִּיק, מָט לִפְנֵי-רָשָׁע

ma'yan nirpas umakor mashechat; tzaddik, mat lifnei-rasha

As a troubled fountain, and a corrupted spring, so is a righteous man that giveth way before the wicked.

אָכֹל דְּבַשׁ הַרְבּוֹת לֹא-טוֹב; וְחֵקֶר כְּבֹדָם כָּבוֹד

'achol devash harbot lo-tov; vecheker kevodam kavod

It is not good to eat much honey; so for men to search out their own glory is not glory.

עִיר פְּרוּצָה, אֵין חוֹמָה--אִישׁ, אֲשֶׁר אֵין מַעְצָר לְרוּחוֹ

'ir perutzah ein chomah; ish, asher ein ma'tzar lerucho

Like a city broken down and without a wall, so is he whose spirit is without restraint.

כו

כַּשֶּׁלֶג, בַּקַּיִץ--וְכַמָּטָר בַּקָּצִיר: כֵּן לֹא-נָאוֶה לִכְסִיל כָּבוֹד

Kasheleg bakkayitz, vechammatar bakkatzir; ken lo-naveh lichsil kavod

As snow in summer, and as rain in harvest, so honour is not seemly for a fool.

אַל-תֵּצֵא לָרִב, מַהֵר: פֶּן מַה-תַּעֲשֶׂה, בְּאַחֲרִיתָהּ--בְּהַכְלִים אֹתְךָ רֵעֶךָ

'al-tetzei lariv, maher pen mah-ta'aseh be'acharitah; behachlim otecha re'echa

Go not forth hastily to strive, lest thou know not what to do in the end thereof, when thy neighbour hath put thee to shame.

רִיבְךָ, רִיב אֶת-רֵעֶךָ; וְסוֹד אַחֵר אַל-תְּגָל

rivecha riv et-re'echa; vesod acher al-tegal

Debate thy cause with thy neighbour, but reveal not the secret of another;

פֶּן-יְחַסֶּדְךָ שֹׁמֵעַ; וְדִבָּתְךָ, לֹא תָשׁוּב

pen-yechassedcha shomea'; vedibbatecha, lo tashuv

Lest he that heareth it revile thee, and thine infamy turn not away.

תַּפּוּחֵי זָהָב, בְּמַשְׂכִּיּוֹת כָּסֶף--דָּבָר, דָּבֻר עַל-אָפְנָיו

tappuchei zahov bemaskiyot kasef; davar, davur al-'afenav

A word fitly spoken is like apples of gold in settings of silver.

נֶזֶם זָהָב, וַחֲלִי-כָתֶם--מוֹכִיחַ חָכָם, עַל-אֹזֶן שֹׁמָעַת

nezem zahov vachali-chatem; mochiach chacham, al-'ozen shoma'at

As an ear-ring of gold, and an ornament of fine gold, so is a wise reprover upon an obedient ear.

כְּצִנַּת שֶׁלֶג, בְּיוֹם קָצִיר--צִיר נֶאֱמָן, לְשֹׁלְחָיו

ketzinnat-sheleg beyom katzir, tzir ne'emon lesholechav

As the cold of snow in the time of harvest, so is a faithful messenger to him that sendeth him;

וְנֶפֶשׁ אֲדֹנָיו יָשִׁיב

venefesh adonav yashiv

for he refresheth the soul of his master.

נְשִׂיאִים וְרוּחַ, וְגֶשֶׁם אָיִן--אִישׁ מִתְהַלֵּל, בְּמַתַּת-שָׁקֶר

nesi'im veruach vegeshem ayin; ish mit'hallel, bemattat-shaker

As vapours and wind without rain, so is he that boasteth himself of a false gift.

בְּאֹרֶךְ אַפַּיִם, יְפֻתֶּה קָצִין; וְלָשׁוֹן רַכָּה, תִּשְׁבָּר-גָּרֶם

be'orech appayim yefutteh katzin; velashon rakkah, tishbor-garem

By long forbearing is a ruler persuaded, and a soft tongue breaketh the bone.

דְּבַשׁ מָצָאתָ, אֱכֹל דַּיֶּךָ: פֶּן-תִּשְׂבָּעֶנּוּ, וַהֲקֵאתוֹ

devash matzata echol dayeka; pen-tisba'ennu, vahaketo

Hast thou found honey? eat so much as is sufficient for thee, lest thou be filled therewith, and vomit it.

הֹקַר רַגְלְךָ, מִבֵּית רֵעֶךָ: פֶּן-יִשְׂבָּעֲךָ, וּשְׂנֵאֶךָ

hokar raglecha mibbeit re'echa; pen-yisba'acha, usene'echa

Let thy foot be seldom in thy neighbour's house; lest he be sated with thee, and hate thee.

מֵפִיץ וְחֶרֶב, וְחֵץ שָׁנוּן--אִישׁ עֹנֶה בְרֵעֵהוּ, עֵד שָׁקֶר

mefitz vecherev vechetz shanun; ish oneh vere'ehu, ed shaker

As a maul, and a sword, and a sharp arrow, so is a man that beareth false witness against his neighbour.

וָאֶחֱזֶה אָנֹכִי, אָשִׁית לִבִּי; רָאִיתִי, לָקַחְתִּי מוּסָר
va'echezeh anochi ashit libbi; ra'iti, lakachti musar
Then I beheld, and considered well; I saw, and received instruction.

מְעַט שֵׁנוֹת, מְעַט תְּנוּמוֹת; מְעַט, חִבֻּק יָדַיִם לִשְׁכָּב
me'at shenot me'at tenumot; me'at chibbuk yadayim lishkav
'Yet a little sleep, a little slumber, a little folding of the hands to sleep'--

וּבָא-מִתְהַלֵּךְ רֵישֶׁךָ; וּמַחְסֹרֶיךָ, כְּאִישׁ מָגֵן
uva-mit'hallech reishecha; umachsoreicha, ke'ish magen
So shall thy poverty come as a runner, and thy want as an armed man.

כה

גַּם-אֵלֶּה, מִשְׁלֵי שְׁלֹמֹה--אֲשֶׁר הֶעְתִּיקוּ, אַנְשֵׁי חִזְקִיָּה מֶלֶךְ-יְהוּדָה
Gam-'elleh mishlei shelomoh; asher he'tiku, anshei chizkiyah melech-yehudah
These also are proverbs of Solomon, which the men of Hezekiah king of Judah copied out.

כְּבֹד אֱלֹהִים, הַסְתֵּר דָּבָר; וּכְבֹד מְלָכִים, חֲקֹר דָּבָר
kevod elohim haster davar; uchevod melachim, chakor davar
It is the glory of God to conceal a thing; but the glory of kings is to search out a matter.

שָׁמַיִם לָרוּם, וָאָרֶץ לָעֹמֶק; וְלֵב מְלָכִים, אֵין חֵקֶר
shamayim larum va'aretz la'omek; velev melachim, ein cheker
The heaven for height, and the earth for depth, and the heart of kings is unsearchable.

הָגוֹ סִיגִים מִכָּסֶף; וַיֵּצֵא לַצֹּרֵף כֶּלִי
hago sigim mikkasef; vayetzei latzoref keli
Take away the dross from the silver, and there cometh forth a vessel for the refiner;

הָגוֹ רָשָׁע, לִפְנֵי-מֶלֶךְ; וְיִכּוֹן בַּצֶּדֶק כִּסְאוֹ
hago rasho lifnei-melech; veyikkon batzedek kis'o
Take away the wicked from before the king, and his throne shall be established in righteousness.

אַל-תִּתְהַדַּר לִפְנֵי-מֶלֶךְ; וּבִמְקוֹם גְּדֹלִים, אַל-תַּעֲמֹד
'al-tit'haddar lifnei-melech; uvimkom gedolim, al-ta'amod
Glorify not thyself in the presence of the king, and stand not in the place of great men;

כִּי טוֹב אֲמָר-לְךָ, עֲלֵה-הֵנָּה
ki tov amar-lecha, aleh hennah
For better is it that it be said unto thee: 'Come up hither',

מֵהַשְׁפִּילְךָ, לִפְנֵי נָדִיב--אֲשֶׁר רָאוּ עֵינֶיךָ
mehashpilecha lifnei nadiv; asher ra'u eineicha
than that thou shouldest be put lower in the presence of the prince, whom thine eyes have seen.

יְרָא-אֶת-יְהוָה בְּנִי וָמֶלֶךְ; עִם-שׁוֹנִים, אַל-תִּתְעָרָב

yera-'et-hashem beni vamelech; im-shonim, al-tit'arav

My son, fear thou the LORD and the king, and meddle not with them that are given to change;

כִּי-פִתְאֹם, יָקוּם אֵידָם; וּפִיד שְׁנֵיהֶם, מִי יוֹדֵעַ

ki-fit'om yakum eidam; ufid sheneihem, mi yodea

For their calamity shall rise suddenly; and who knoweth the ruin from them both?

גַּם-אֵלֶּה לַחֲכָמִים: הַכֵּר-פָּנִים בְּמִשְׁפָּט בַּל-טוֹב

gam-'elleh lachachamim; hakker-panim bemishpat bal-tov

These also are sayings of the wise. To have respect of persons in judgment is not good.

אֹמֵר, לְרָשָׁע--צַדִּיק אָתָּה: יִקְּבֻהוּ עַמִּים; יִזְעָמוּהוּ לְאֻמִּים

'omer lerasha tzaddik attah yikkevuhu ammim; yiz'amuhu le'ummim

He that saith unto the wicked: 'Thou art righteous', peoples shall curse him, nations shall execrate him;

וְלַמּוֹכִיחִים יִנְעָם; וַעֲלֵיהֶם, תָּבוֹא בִרְכַּת-טוֹב

velammochichim yin'am; va'aleihem, tavo virkat-tov

But to them that decide justly shall be delight, and a good blessing shall come upon them.

שְׂפָתַיִם יִשָּׁק; מֵשִׁיב, דְּבָרִים נְכֹחִים

sefatayim yishak; meshiv, devarim nechochim

He kisseth the lips that giveth a right answer.

הָכֵן בַּחוּץ, מְלַאכְתֶּךָ--וְעַתְּדָהּ בַּשָּׂדֶה לָךְ; אַחַר, וּבָנִיתָ בֵיתֶךָ

hachen bachutz melachtecha, ve'attedah bassadeh lach; achar, uvanita veitecha

Prepare thy work without, and make it fit for thyself in the field; and afterwards build thy house.

אַל-תְּהִי עֵד-חִנָּם בְּרֵעֶךָ; וַהֲפִתִּיתָ, בִּשְׂפָתֶיךָ

'al-tehi ed-chinnam bere'echa; vahafittita, bisfateicha

Be not a witness against thy neighbour without cause; and deceive not with thy lips.

אַל-תֹּאמַר--כַּאֲשֶׁר עָשָׂה-לִי, כֵּן אֶעֱשֶׂה-לּוֹ; אָשִׁיב לָאִישׁ כְּפָעֳלוֹ

'al-tomar, ka'asher asah-li ken e'eseh-lo; ashiv la'ish kefo'olo

Say not: 'I will do so to him as he hath done to me; I will render to the man according to his work.'

עַל-שְׂדֵה אִישׁ-עָצֵל עָבַרְתִּי; וְעַל-כֶּרֶם, אָדָם חֲסַר-לֵב

'al-sedeh ish-'atzel avarti; ve'al-kerem, adam chasar-lev

I went by the field of the slothful, and by the vineyard of the man void of understanding;

וְהִנֵּה עָלָה כֻלּוֹ, קִמְּשֹׂנִים

vehinneh alah chullo kimmesonim

And, lo, it was all grown over with thistles,

כָּסּוּ פָנָיו חֲרֻלִּים; וְגֶדֶר אֲבָנָיו נֶהֱרָסָה

kassu fanav charullim; vegeder avanav neherasah

the face thereof was covered with nettles, and the stone wall thereof was broken down.

הִתְרַפִּיתָ, בְּיוֹם צָרָה--צַר כֹּחֶכָה
hitrappita beyom tzarah, tzar kochechah
If thou faint in the day of adversity, thy strength is small indeed.

הַצֵּל, לְקֻחִים לַמָּוֶת; וּמָטִים לַהֶרֶג, אִם-תַּחְשׂוֹךְ
hatzel lekuchim lammavet; umatim lahereg, im-tachsoch
Deliver them that are drawn unto death; and those that are ready to be slain wilt thou forbear to rescue?

כִּי-תֹאמַר--הֵן, לֹא-יָדַעְנוּ-זֶה: הֲלֹא-תֹכֵן לִבּוֹת, הוּא-יָבִין
ki-tomar, hen lo-yada'nu zeh halo-tochen libbot hu-yavin
If thou sayest: 'Behold, we knew not this', doth not He that weigheth the hearts consider it?

וְנֹצֵר נַפְשְׁךָ, הוּא יֵדָע; וְהֵשִׁיב לְאָדָם כְּפָעֳלוֹ
venotzer nafshecha hu yeda'; veheshiv le'adam kefo'olo
And He that keepeth thy soul, doth not He know it? And shall not He render to every man according to his works?

אֱכָל-בְּנִי דְבַשׁ כִּי-טוֹב; וְנֹפֶת מָתוֹק, עַל-חִכֶּךָ
'echal-beni devash ki-tov; venofet matok, al-chikkecha
My son, eat thou honey, for it is good, and the honeycomb is sweet to thy taste;

כֵּן, דְּעֶה חָכְמָה--לְנַפְשֶׁךָ: אִם-מָצָאתָ, וְיֵשׁ אַחֲרִית; וְתִקְוָתְךָ, לֹא תִכָּרֵת
ken de'eh chochmah lenafshecha im-matzata veyesh acharit; vetikvatecha, lo tikkaret
So know thou wisdom to be unto thy soul; if thou hast found it, then shall there be a future, and thy hope shall not be cut off.

אַל-תֶּאֱרֹב רָשָׁע, לִנְוֵה צַדִּיק; אַל-תְּשַׁדֵּד רִבְצוֹ
'al-te'erov rasha linveh tzaddik; al-teshadded rivtzo
Lie not in wait, O wicked man, against the dwelling of the righteous, spoil not his resting-place;

כִּי שֶׁבַע, יִפּוֹל צַדִּיק וָקָם; וּרְשָׁעִים, יִכָּשְׁלוּ בְרָעָה
ki sheva yippol tzaddik vakam; uresha'im, yikkashelu vera'ah
For a righteous man falleth seven times, and riseth up again, but the wicked stumble under adversity.

בִּנְפֹל אוֹיִבְךָ, אַל-תִּשְׂמָח; וּבִכָּשְׁלוֹ, אַל-יָגֵל לִבֶּךָ
binfol oyivcha al-tismach; uvikkashelo, al-yagel libbecha
Rejoice not when thine enemy falleth, and let not thy heart be glad when he stumbleth;

פֶּן-יִרְאֶה יְהוָה, וְרַע בְּעֵינָיו; וְהֵשִׁיב מֵעָלָיו אַפּוֹ
pen-yir'eh hashem vera be'einav; veheshiv me'alav appo
Lest the LORD see it, and it displease Him, and He turn away His wrath from him.

אַל-תִּתְחַר בַּמְּרֵעִים; אַל-תְּקַנֵּא, בָּרְשָׁעִים
'al-titchar bammere'im; al-tekanne, baresha'im
Fret not thyself because of evildoers, neither be thou envious at the wicked;

כִּי, לֹא-תִהְיֶה אַחֲרִית לָרָע; נֵר רְשָׁעִים יִדְעָךְ
ki lo-tihyeh acharit lara'; ner resha'im yid'ach
For there will be no future to the evil man, the lamp of the wicked shall be put out.

הִכּוּנִי בַל-חָלִיתִי--הֲלָמוּנִי, בַּל-יָדָעְתִּי

hikkuni val-chaliti halamuni, bal-yada'eti

'They have struck me, and I felt it not, they have beaten me, and I knew it not;

מָתַי אָקִיץ; אוֹסִיף, אֲבַקְשֶׁנּוּ עוֹד

matai akitz; osif, avakshennu od

when shall I awake? I will seek it yet again.'

כד

אַל-תְּקַנֵּא, בְּאַנְשֵׁי רָעָה; וְאַל-תִּתְאָו, לִהְיוֹת אִתָּם

Al-tekannei be'anshei ra'ah; ve'al-tit'av ve'al-tit'av, lihyot ittam

Be not thou envious of evil men, neither desire to be with them.

כִּי-שֹׁד, יֶהְגֶּה לִבָּם; וְעָמָל, שִׂפְתֵיהֶם תְּדַבֵּרְנָה

ki-shod yehgeh libbam; ve'amal, sifteihem tedabbernah

For their heart studieth destruction, and their lips talk of mischief.

בְּחָכְמָה, יִבָּנֶה בָּיִת; וּבִתְבוּנָה, יִתְכּוֹנָן

bechochmah yibbaneh bayit; uvitvunah, yitkonan

Through wisdom is a house builded; and by understanding it is established;

וּבְדַעַת, חֲדָרִים יִמָּלְאוּ--כָּל-הוֹן יָקָר וְנָעִים

uveda'at chadarim yimmale'u; kol-hon yakar vena'im

And by knowledge are the chambers filled with all precious and pleasant riches.

גֶּבֶר-חָכָם בַּעוֹז; וְאִישׁ-דַּעַת, מְאַמֶּץ-כֹּחַ

gever-chacham ba'oz; ve'ish-da'at, me'ammetz-koach

A wise man is strong; yea, a man of knowledge increaseth strength.

כִּי בְתַחְבֻּלוֹת, תַּעֲשֶׂה-לְּךָ מִלְחָמָה; וּתְשׁוּעָה, בְּרֹב יוֹעֵץ

ki vetachbulot ta'aseh-lecha milchamah; uteshu'ah, berov yo'etz

For with wise advice thou shalt make thy war; and in the multitude of counsellors there is safety.

רָאמוֹת לֶאֱוִיל חָכְמוֹת; בַּשַּׁעַר, לֹא יִפְתַּח-פִּיהוּ

ramot le'evil chochemot; basha'ar, lo yiftach-pihu

Wisdom is as unattainable to a fool as corals; he openeth not his mouth in the gate.

מְחַשֵּׁב לְהָרֵעַ--לוֹ, בַּעַל-מְזִמּוֹת יִקְרָאוּ

mechashev leharea'; lo, ba'al-mezimmot yikra'u

He that deviseth to do evil, men shall call him a mischievous person.

זִמַּת אִוֶּלֶת חַטָּאת; וְתוֹעֲבַת לְאָדָם לֵץ

zimmat ivvelet chattat; veto'avat le'adam letz

The thought of foolishness is sin; and the scorner is an abomination to men.

גִּיל יָגִיל, אֲבִי צַדִּיק; וְיוֹלֵד חָכָם, יִשְׂמַח-בּוֹ

gil yagol yagil avi tzaddik; veyoled chacham, yismach-bo

The father of the righteous will greatly rejoice; and he that begetteth a wise child will have joy of him.

יִשְׂמַח-אָבִיךָ וְאִמֶּךָ; וְתָגֵל, יוֹלַדְתֶּךָ

yismach-'avicha ve'immecha; vetagel, yoladtecha

Let thy father and thy mother be glad, and let her that bore thee rejoice.

תְּנָה-בְנִי לִבְּךָ לִי; וְעֵינֶיךָ, דְּרָכַי תִּצֹּרְנָה

tenah-veni libbecha li; ve'eineicha, derachai titzorenah

My son, give me thy heart, and let thine eyes observe my ways.

כִּי-שׁוּחָה עֲמֻקָּה זוֹנָה; וּבְאֵר צָרָה, נָכְרִיָּה

ki-shuchah amukkah zonah; uve'er tzarah, nocheriyah

For a harlot is a deep ditch; and an alien woman is a narrow pit.

אַף-הִיא, כְּחֶתֶף תֶּאֱרֹב; וּבוֹגְדִים, בְּאָדָם תּוֹסִף

'af-hi kechetef te'erov; uvogedim, be'adam tosif

She also lieth in wait as a robber, and increaseth the faithless among men.

לְמִי אוֹי לְמִי אֲבוֹי, לְמִי מִדְיָנִים לְמִי שִׂיחַ

lemi oy lemi avoy lemi midyanim lemi siach

Who crieth: 'Woe'? who: 'Alas'? who hath contentions? who hath raving?

לְמִי, פְּצָעִים חִנָּם; לְמִי, חַכְלִלוּת עֵינָיִם

lemi petza'im chinnam; lemi, chachlilut einayim

Who hath wounds without cause? Who hath redness of eyes?

לַמְאַחֲרִים עַל-הַיָּיִן--לַבָּאִים, לַחְקֹר מִמְסָךְ

lam'acharim al-hayayin; labba'im, lachkor mimsach

They that tarry long at the wine; they that go to try mixed wine.

אַל-תֵּרֶא יַיִן, כִּי יִתְאַדָּם: כִּי-יִתֵּן בַּכּוֹס עֵינוֹ; יִתְהַלֵּךְ, בְּמֵישָׁרִים

'al-terei yayin ki yit'addam ki-yitten bakkos eino; yit'hallech, bemeisharim

Look not thou upon the wine when it is red, when it giveth its colour in the cup, when it glideth down smoothly;

אַחֲרִיתוֹ, כְּנָחָשׁ יִשָּׁךְ; וּכְצִפְעֹנִי יַפְרִשׁ

'acharito kenachash yishach; uchetzif'oni yafrish

At the last it biteth like a serpent, and stingeth like a basilisk.

עֵינֶיךָ, יִרְאוּ זָרוֹת; וְלִבְּךָ, יְדַבֵּר תַּהְפֻּכוֹת

'eineicha yir'u zarot; velibbecha, yedabber tahpuchot

Thine eyes shall behold strange things, and thy heart shall utter confused things.

וְהָיִיתָ, כְּשֹׁכֵב בְּלֶב-יָם; וּכְשֹׁכֵב, בְּרֹאשׁ חִבֵּל

vehayita keshochev belev-yam; ucheshochev, berosh chibbel

Yea, thou shalt be as he that lieth down in the midst of the sea, or as he that lieth upon the top of a mast.

הָבִיאָה לַמּוּסָר לִבֶּךָ; וְאָזְנֶךָ, לְאִמְרֵי-דָעַת
havi'ah lammusar libbecha; ve'azenecha, le'imrei-da'at
Apply thy heart unto instruction, and thine ears to the words of knowledge.

אַל-תִּמְנַע מִנַּעַר מוּסָר: כִּי-תַכֶּנּוּ בַשֵּׁבֶט, לֹא יָמוּת
'al-timna minna'ar musar; ki-takkennu vashevet, lo yamut
Withhold not correction from the child; for though thou beat him with the rod, he will not die.

אַתָּה, בַּשֵּׁבֶט תַּכֶּנּוּ; וְנַפְשׁוֹ, מִשְּׁאוֹל תַּצִּיל
'attah bashevet takkennu; venafsho, mishe'ol tatzil
Thou beatest him with the rod, and wilt deliver his soul from the nether-world.

בְּנִי, אִם-חָכַם לִבֶּךָ--יִשְׂמַח לִבִּי גַם-אָנִי
beni im-chacham libbecha; yismach libbi gam-'ani
My son, if thy heart be wise, my heart will be glad, even mine;

וְתַעְלֹזְנָה כִלְיוֹתָי--בְּדַבֵּר שְׂפָתֶיךָ, מֵישָׁרִים
veta'lozenah chilyotai; bedabber sefateicha, meisharim
Yea, my reins will rejoice, when thy lips speak right things.

אַל-יְקַנֵּא לִבְּךָ, בַּחַטָּאִים: כִּי אִם-בְּיִרְאַת-יְהוָה, כָּל-הַיּוֹם
'al-yekannei libbecha bachatta'im; ki im-beyir'at-hashem kol-hayom
Let not thy heart envy sinners, but be in the fear of the LORD all the day;

כִּי, אִם-יֵשׁ אַחֲרִית; וְתִקְוָתְךָ, לֹא תִכָּרֵת
ki im-yesh acharit; vetikvatecha, lo tikkaret
For surely there is a future; and thy hope shall not be cut off.

שְׁמַע-אַתָּה בְנִי וַחֲכָם; וְאַשֵּׁר בַּדֶּרֶךְ לִבֶּךָ
shema'-'attah veni vachacham; ve'asher badderech libbecha
Hear thou, my son, and be wise, and guide thy heart in the way.

אַל-תְּהִי בְסֹבְאֵי-יָיִן--בְּזֹלְלֵי בָשָׂר לָמוֹ
'al-tehi vesove'ei-yayin; bezolalei vasar lamo
Be not among winebibbers; among gluttonous eaters of flesh;

כִּי-סֹבֵא וְזוֹלֵל, יִוָּרֵשׁ; וּקְרָעִים, תַּלְבִּישׁ נוּמָה
ki-sovei vezolel yivvaresh; ukera'im, talbish numah
For the drunkard and the glutton shall come to poverty; and drowsiness shall clothe a man with rags.

שְׁמַע לְאָבִיךָ, זֶה יְלָדֶךָ; וְאַל-תָּבוּז, כִּי-זָקְנָה אִמֶּךָ
shema le'avicha zeh yeladecha; ve'al-tavuz, ki-zakenah immecha
Hearken unto thy father that begot thee, and despise not thy mother when she is old.

אֱמֶת קְנֵה, וְאַל-תִּמְכֹּר; חָכְמָה וּמוּסָר וּבִינָה
'emet keneh ve'al-timkor; chochmah umusar uvinah
Buy the truth, and sell it not; also wisdom, and instruction, and understanding.

כג

כִּי-תֵשֵׁב, לִלְחוֹם אֶת-מוֹשֵׁל--בִּין תָּבִין, אֶת-אֲשֶׁר לְפָנֶיךָ
Ki-teshev lilchom et-moshel; bin tavin, et-'asher lefaneicha
When thou sittest to eat with a ruler, consider well him that is before thee;

וְשַׂמְתָּ שַׂכִּין בְּלֹעֶךָ--אִם-בַּעַל נֶפֶשׁ אַתָּה
vesamta sakkin belo'echa; im-ba'al nefesh attah
And put a knife to thy throat, if thou be a man given to appetite.

אַל-תִּתְאָו, לְמַטְעַמּוֹתָיו; וְהוּא, לֶחֶם כְּזָבִים
'al-tit'ov lemat'ammotav; vehu, lechem kezavim
Be not desirous of his dainties; seeing they are deceitful food.

אַל-תִּיגַע לְהַעֲשִׁיר; מִבִּינָתְךָ חֲדָל
'al-tiga leha'ashir; mibbinatecha chadal
Weary not thyself to be rich; cease from thine own wisdom.

הֲתָעִיף עֵינֶיךָ בּוֹ, וְאֵינֶנּוּ: כִּי עָשֹׂה יַעֲשֶׂה-לּוֹ כְנָפַיִם; כְּנֶשֶׁר, יָעוּף הַשָּׁמָיִם
hata'if eineicha bo, ve'einennu ki asoh ya'aseh-lo chenafayim; kenesher, ya'uf hashamayim
Wilt thou set thine eyes upon it? it is gone; for riches certainly make themselves wings, like an eagle that flieth toward heaven.

אַל-תִּלְחַם--אֶת-לֶחֶם, רַע עָיִן; וְאַל-תִּתְאָו, לְמַטְעַמֹּתָיו
'al-tilcham, et-lechem ra ayin; ve'al-tit'av, lemat'ammotav
Eat thou not the bread of him that hath an evil eye, neither desire thou his dainties;

כִּי, כְּמוֹ שָׁעַר בְּנַפְשׁוֹ--כֶּן-הוּא: אֱכֹל וּשְׁתֵה, יֹאמַר לָךְ; וְלִבּוֹ, בַּל-עִמָּךְ
ki kemo-sha'ar benafsho, ken-hu echol usheteh yomar lach; velibbo, bal-'immach
For as one that hath reckoned within himself, so is he: 'Eat and drink', saith he to thee; but his heart is not with thee.

פִּתְּךָ-אָכַלְתָּ תְקִיאֶנָּה; וְשִׁחַתָּ, דְּבָרֶיךָ הַנְּעִימִים
pittecha-'achalta teki'ennah; veshichata, devareicha hanne'imim
The morsel which thou hast eaten shalt thou vomit up, and lose thy sweet words.

בְּאָזְנֵי כְסִיל, אַל-תְּדַבֵּר: כִּי-יָבוּז, לְשֵׂכֶל מִלֶּיךָ
be'ozenei chesil al-tedabber; ki-yavuz, lesechel milleicha
Speak not in the ears of a fool; for he will despise the wisdom of thy words.

אַל-תַּסֵּג, גְּבוּל עוֹלָם; וּבִשְׂדֵי יְתוֹמִים, אַל-תָּבֹא
'al-tasseg gevul olam; uvisdei yetomim, al-tavo
Remove not the ancient landmark; and enter not into the fields of the fatherless;

כִּי-גֹאֲלָם חָזָק; הוּא-יָרִיב אֶת-רִיבָם אִתָּךְ
ki-go'alam chazak; hu-yariv et-rivam ittach
For their Redeemer is strong; He will plead their cause with thee.

הֲלֹא כָתַבְתִּי לְךָ, שָׁלִשִׁים--בְּמֹעֵצוֹת וָדָעַת
halo chatavti lecha shalishim; bemo'etzot vada'at
Have not I written unto thee excellent things of counsels and knowledge;

לְהוֹדִיעֲךָ--קֹשְׁטְ, אִמְרֵי אֱמֶת
lehodi'acha, kosht imrei emet;
That I might make thee know the certainty of the words of truth,

לְהָשִׁיב אֲמָרִים אֱמֶת, לְשֹׁלְחֶיךָ
lehashiv amarim emet, lesholecheicha
that thou mightest bring back words of truth to them that send thee?

אַל-תִּגְזָל-דָּל, כִּי דַל-הוּא; וְאַל-תְּדַכֵּא עָנִי בַשָּׁעַר
'al-tigzal-dal ki dal-hu; ve'al-tedakkei ani vasha'ar
Rob not the weak, because he is weak, neither crush the poor in the gate;

כִּי-יְהוָה, יָרִיב רִיבָם; וְקָבַע אֶת-קֹבְעֵיהֶם נָפֶשׁ
ki-hashem yariv rivam; vekava et-kove'eihem nafesh
For the LORD will plead their cause, and despoil of life those that despoil them.

אַל-תִּתְרַע, אֶת-בַּעַל אָף; וְאֶת-אִישׁ חֵמוֹת, לֹא תָבוֹא
'al-titra et-ba'al af; ve'et-'ish chemot lo tavo
Make no friendship with a man that is given to anger; and with a wrathful man thou shalt not go;

פֶּן-תֶּאֱלַף אֹרְחֹתָו; וְלָקַחְתָּ מוֹקֵשׁ לְנַפְשֶׁךָ
pen-te'elaf orechotav; velakachta mokesh lenafshecha
Lest thou learn his ways, and get a snare to thy soul.

אַל-תְּהִי בְתֹקְעֵי-כָף; בַּעֹרְבִים, מַשָּׁאוֹת
'al-tehi vetoke'ei-chaf; ba'orevim, masha'ot
Be thou not of them that strike hands, or of them that are sureties for debts;

אִם-אֵין-לְךָ לְשַׁלֵּם--לָמָּה יִקַּח מִשְׁכָּבְךָ, מִתַּחְתֶּיךָ
'im-'ein-lecha leshallem; lammah yikkach mishkavecha, mittachteicha
If thou hast not wherewith to pay, why should he take away thy bed from under thee?

אַל-תַּסֵּג, גְּבוּל עוֹלָם--אֲשֶׁר עָשׂוּ אֲבוֹתֶיךָ
'al-tasseg gevul olam; asher asu avoteicha
Remove not the ancient landmark, which thy fathers have set.

חָזִיתָ אִישׁ, מָהִיר בִּמְלַאכְתּוֹ--לִפְנֵי-מְלָכִים יִתְיַצָּב; בַּל-יִתְיַצֵּב, לִפְנֵי חֲשֻׁכִּים
chazita ish mahir bimlachto, lifnei-melachim yityatzav; bal-yityatzev lifnei chashukkim
Seest thou a man diligent in his business? he shall stand before kings; he shall not stand before mean men.

זוֹרֵעַ עַוְלָה, יִקְצָר-אָוֶן; וְשֵׁבֶט עֶבְרָתוֹ יִכְלֶה

zorea avlah yiktzar-'aven; veshevet evrato yichleh

He that soweth iniquity shall reap vanity; and the rod of his wrath shall fail.

טוֹב-עַיִן, הוּא יְבֹרָךְ: כִּי-נָתַן מִלַּחְמוֹ לַדָּל

tov-'ayin hu yevorach; ki-natan millachmo laddal

He that hath a bountiful eye shall be blessed; for he giveth of his bread to the poor.

גָּרֵשׁ לֵץ, וְיֵצֵא מָדוֹן; וְיִשְׁבֹּת, דִּין וְקָלוֹן.

garesh letz veyetzei madon; veyishbot, din vekalon

Cast out the scorner, and contention will go out; yea, strife and shame will cease.

אֹהֵב טְהָר-לֵב--חֵן שְׂפָתָיו, רֵעֵהוּ מֶלֶךְ

'ohev tehar-lev; chen sefatav, re'ehu melech

He that loveth pureness of heart, that hath grace in his lips, the king shall be his friend.

עֵינֵי יְהוָה, נָצְרוּ דָעַת; וַיְסַלֵּף, דִּבְרֵי בֹגֵד

'einei hashem natzeru da'at; vaysallef, divrei voged

The eyes of the LORD preserve him that hath knowledge, but He overthroweth the words of the faithless man.

אָמַר עָצֵל, אֲרִי בַחוּץ; בְּתוֹךְ רְחֹבוֹת, אֵרָצֵחַ

'amar atzel ari vachutz; betoch rechovot, eratzeach

The sluggard saith: 'There is a lion without; I shall be slain in the streets.'

שׁוּחָה עֲמֻקָּה, פִּי זָרוֹת; זְעוּם יְהוָה, יִפָּל-שָׁם

shuchah amukkah pi zarot; ze'um hashem yippal-sham

The mouth of strange women is a deep pit: he that is abhorred of the LORD shall fall therein.

אִוֶּלֶת, קְשׁוּרָה בְלֶב-נָעַר; שֵׁבֶט מוּסָר, יַרְחִיקֶנָּה מִמֶּנּוּ

'ivvelet keshurah velev-na'ar; shevet musar, yarchikennah mimmennu

Foolishness is bound up in the heart of a child; but the rod of correction shall drive it far from him.

עֹשֵׁק דָּל, לְהַרְבּוֹת לוֹ--נֹתֵן לְעָשִׁיר, אַךְ-לְמַחְסוֹר

'oshek dal leharbot lo; noten le'ashir, ach-lemachsor

One may oppress the poor, yet will their gain increase; one may give to the rich, yet will want come.

הַט אָזְנְךָ--וּשְׁמַע, דִּבְרֵי חֲכָמִים; וְלִבְּךָ, תָּשִׁית לְדַעְתִּי

hat ozenecha, ushema divrei chachamim; velibbecha, tashit leda'ti

Incline thine ear, and hear the words of the wise, and apply thy heart unto my knowledge.

כִּי-נָעִים, כִּי-תִשְׁמְרֵם בְּבִטְנֶךָ; יִכֹּנוּ יַחְדָּו, עַל-שְׂפָתֶיךָ

ki-na'im ki-tishmerem bevitnecha; yikkonu yachdav, al-sefateicha

For it is a pleasant thing if thou keep them within thee; let them be established altogether upon thy lips.

לִהְיוֹת בַּיהוָה, מִבְטַחֶךָ--הוֹדַעְתִּיךָ הַיּוֹם אַף-אָתָּה

lihyot bahashem mivtachecha; hoda'ticha hayom af-'attah

That thy trust may be in the LORD, I have made them known to thee this day, even to thee.

עֵד-כְּזָבִים יֹאבֵד; וְאִישׁ שׁוֹמֵעַ, לָנֶצַח יְדַבֵּר

'ed-kezavim yoved; ve'ish shomea', lanetzach yedabber

A false witness shall perish; but the man that obeyeth shall speak unchallenged.

הֵעֵז אִישׁ רָשָׁע בְּפָנָיו; וְיָשָׁר, הוּא יָבִין דַּרְכּוֹ

he'ez ish rasha befanav; veyashar, hu yavin darko

A wicked man hardeneth his face; but as for the upright, he looketh well to his way.

אֵין חָכְמָה, וְאֵין תְּבוּנָה--וְאֵין עֵצָה, לְנֶגֶד יְהוָה

'ein chochmah ve'ein tevunah; ve'ein etzah, leneged hashem

There is no wisdom nor understanding nor counsel against the LORD.

סוּס--מוּכָן, לְיוֹם מִלְחָמָה; וְלַיהוָה, הַתְּשׁוּעָה

sus, muchon leyom milchamah; velahashem, hatteshu'ah

The horse is prepared against the day of battle; but victory is of the LORD.

כב

נִבְחָר שֵׁם, מֵעֹשֶׁר רָב: מִכֶּסֶף וּמִזָּהָב, חֵן טוֹב

Nivchar shem me'osher rav; mikkesef umizzahav, chen tov

A good name is rather to be chosen than great riches, and loving favour rather than silver and gold.

עָשִׁיר וָרָשׁ נִפְגָּשׁוּ; עֹשֵׂה כֻלָּם יְהוָה

'ashir varash nifgashu; oseh chullam hashem

The rich and the poor meet together--the LORD is the maker of them all.

עָרוּם, רָאָה רָעָה וְנִסְתָּר; וּפְתָיִים, עָבְרוּ וְנֶעֱנָשׁוּ

'arum ra'ah ra'ah venistar; ufetayim, averu vene'enashu

A prudent man seeth the evil, and hideth himself; but the thoughtless pass on, and are punished.

עֵקֶב עֲנָוָה, יִרְאַת יְהוָה; עֹשֶׁר וְכָבוֹד וְחַיִּים

'ekev anavah yir'at hashem osher vechavod vechayim

The reward of humility is the fear of the LORD, even riches, and honour, and life.

צִנִּים פַּחִים, בְּדֶרֶךְ עִקֵּשׁ; שׁוֹמֵר נַפְשׁוֹ, יִרְחַק מֵהֶם

tzinnim pachim bederech ikkesh; shomer nafsho, yirchak mehem

Thorns and snares are in the way of the froward; he that keepeth his soul holdeth himself far from them.

חֲנֹךְ לַנַּעַר, עַל-פִּי דַרְכּוֹ--גַּם כִּי-יַזְקִין, לֹא-יָסוּר מִמֶּנָּה

chanoch lanna'ar al-pi darko; gam ki-yazkin, lo-yasur mimmennah

Train up a child in the way he should go, and even when he is old, he will not depart from it.

עָשִׁיר, בְּרָשִׁים יִמְשׁוֹל; וְעֶבֶד לֹוֶה, לְאִישׁ מַלְוֶה

'ashir berashim yimshol; ve'eved loveh, le'ish malveh

The rich ruleth over the poor, and the borrower is servant to the lender.

אִישׁ מַחְסוֹר, אֹהֵב שִׂמְחָה; אֹהֵב יַיִן-וָשֶׁמֶן, לֹא יַעֲשִׁיר

'ish machsor ohev simchah; ohev yayin-vashemen, lo ya'ashir

He that loveth pleasure shall be a poor man; he that loveth wine and oil shall not be rich.

כֹּפֶר לַצַּדִּיק רָשָׁע; וְתַחַת יְשָׁרִים בּוֹגֵד

kofer latzaddik rasha'; vetachat yesharim boged

The wicked is a ransom for the righteous; and the faithless cometh in the stead of the upright.

טוֹב, שֶׁבֶת בְּאֶרֶץ-מִדְבָּר--מֵאֵשֶׁת מִדְיָנִים וָכָעַס

tov, shevet be'eretz-midbar; me'eshet midyanim vacha'as

It is better to dwell in a desert land, than with a contentious and fretful woman.

אוֹצָר, נֶחְמָד וָשֶׁמֶן--בִּנְוֵה חָכָם; וּכְסִיל אָדָם יְבַלְּעֶנּוּ

'otzar nechmad vashemen binveh chacham; uchesil adam yevalle'ennu

There is desirable treasure and oil in the dwelling of the wise; but a foolish man swalloweth it up.

רֹדֵף, צְדָקָה וָחָסֶד--יִמְצָא חַיִּים, צְדָקָה וְכָבוֹד

rodef tzedakah vachased; yimtza chayim, tzedakah vechavod

He that followeth after righteousness and mercy findeth life, prosperity, and honour.

עִיר גִּבֹּרִים, עָלָה חָכָם; וַיֹּרֶד, עֹז מִבְטֶחָה

'ir gibborim alah chacham; vayored, oz mivtechah

A wise man scaleth the city of the mighty, and bringeth down the stronghold wherein it trusteth.

שֹׁמֵר פִּיו, וּלְשׁוֹנוֹ--שֹׁמֵר מִצָּרוֹת נַפְשׁוֹ

shomer piv uleshono; shomer mitzarot nafsho

Whoso keepeth his mouth and his tongue keepeth his soul from troubles.

זֵד יָהִיר, לֵץ שְׁמוֹ--עוֹשֶׂה, בְּעֶבְרַת זָדוֹן

zed yahir letz shemo; oseh, be'evrat zadon

A proud and haughty man, scorner is his name, even he that dealeth in overbearing pride.

תַּאֲוַת עָצֵל תְּמִיתֶנּוּ: כִּי-מֵאֲנוּ יָדָיו לַעֲשׂוֹת

ta'avat atzel temitennu; ki-me'anu yadav la'asot

The desire of the slothful killeth him; for his hands refuse to labour.

כָּל-הַיּוֹם, הִתְאַוָּה תַאֲוָה; וְצַדִּיק יִתֵּן, וְלֹא יַחְשֹׂךְ

kol-hayom hit'avvah ta'avah; vetzaddik yitten, velo yachsoch

There is that coveteth greedily all the day long; but the righteous giveth and spareth not.

זֶבַח רְשָׁעִים, תּוֹעֵבָה

zevach resha'im to'evah

The sacrifice of the wicked is an abomination;

אַף, כִּי-בְזִמָּה יְבִיאֶנּוּ

af, ki-vezimmah yevi'ennu

how much more, when he bringeth it with the proceeds of wickedness?

מַחְשְׁבוֹת חָרוּץ, אַךְ-לְמוֹתָר; וְכָל-אָץ, אַךְ-לְמַחְסוֹר
machshevot charutz ach-lemotar; vechol-'atz, ach-lemachsor
The thoughts of the diligent tend only to plenteousness; but every one that is hasty hasteth only to want.

פֹּעַל אֹצָרוֹת, בִּלְשׁוֹן שָׁקֶר--הֶבֶל נִדָּף, מְבַקְשֵׁי-מָוֶת
po'al otzarot bilshon shaker; hevel niddaf, mevakshei-mavet
The getting of treasures by a lying tongue is a vapour driven to and fro; they [that seek them] seek death.

שֹׁד-רְשָׁעִים יְגוֹרֵם: כִּי מֵאֲנוּ, לַעֲשׂוֹת מִשְׁפָּט
shod-resha'im yegorem; ki me'anu, la'asot mishpat
The violence of the wicked shall drag them away; because they refuse to do justly.

הֲפַכְפַּךְ דֶּרֶךְ אִישׁ וָזָר; וְזַךְ, יָשָׁר פָּעֳלוֹ
hafachpach derech ish vazar; vezach, yashar po'olo
The way of man is froward and strange; but as for the pure, his work is right.

טוֹב, לָשֶׁבֶת עַל-פִּנַּת-גָּג--מֵאֵשֶׁת מִדְיָנִים, וּבֵית חָבֶר
tov, lashevet al-pinnat-gag; me'eshet midyanim, uveit chaver
It is better to dwell in a corner of the housetop, than in a house in common with a contentious woman.

נֶפֶשׁ רָשָׁע, אִוְּתָה-רָע; לֹא-יֻחַן בְּעֵינָיו רֵעֵהוּ
nefesh rasho ivvetah-ra'; lo-yuchan be'einav re'ehu
The soul of the wicked desireth evil; his neighbour findeth no favour in his eyes.

בַּעֲנָשׁ-לֵץ, יֶחְכַּם-פֶּתִי; וּבְהַשְׂכִּיל לְחָכָם, יִקַּח-דָּעַת
ba'nosh-letz yechkam-peti; uvehaskil lechacham, yikkach-da'at
When the scorner is punished, the thoughtless is made wise; and when the wise is instructed, he receiveth knowledge.

מַשְׂכִּיל צַדִּיק, לְבֵית רָשָׁע; מְסַלֵּף רְשָׁעִים לָרָע
maskil tzaddik leveit rasha'; mesallef resha'im lara
The Righteous One considereth the house of the wicked; overthrowing the wicked to their ruin.

אֹטֵם אָזְנוֹ, מִזַּעֲקַת-דָּל--גַּם-הוּא יִקְרָא, וְלֹא יֵעָנֶה
'otem azeno mizza'akat-dal; gam-hu yikra, velo ye'aneh
Whoso stoppeth his ears at the cry of the poor, he also shall cry himself, but shall not be answered.

מַתָּן בַּסֵּתֶר, יִכְפֶּה-אָף; וְשֹׁחַד בַּחֵק, חֵמָה עַזָּה
mattan basseter yichpeh-'af; veshochad bachek, chemah azzah
A gift in secret pacifieth anger, and a present in the bosom strong wrath.

שִׂמְחָה לַצַּדִּיק, עֲשׂוֹת מִשְׁפָּט; וּמְחִתָּה, לְפֹעֲלֵי אָוֶן
simchah latzaddik asot mishpat; umechittah, lefo'alei aven
To do justly is joy to the righteous, but ruin to the workers of iniquity.

אָדָם--תּוֹעֶה, מִדֶּרֶךְ הַשְׂכֵּל: בִּקְהַל רְפָאִים יָנוּחַ
'adam, to'eh midderech haskel; bik'hal refa'im yanuach
The man that strayeth out of the way of understanding shall rest in the congregation of the shades.

מֵיְהוָה מִצְעֲדֵי-גָבֶר; וְאָדָם, מַה-יָּבִין דַּרְכּוֹ
mehashem mitz'adei-gaver; ve'adam, mah-yavin darko
A man's goings are of the LORD; how then can man look to his way?

מוֹקֵשׁ אָדָם, יָלַע קֹדֶשׁ; וְאַחַר נְדָרִים לְבַקֵּר
mokesh adom yala kodesh; ve'achar nedarim levakker
It is a snare to a man rashly to say: 'Holy', and after vows to make inquiry.

מְזָרֶה רְשָׁעִים, מֶלֶךְ חָכָם; וַיָּשֶׁב עֲלֵיהֶם אוֹפָן
mezareh resha'im melech chacham; vayashev aleihem ofan
A wise king sifteth the wicked, and turneth the wheel over them.

נֵר יְהוָה, נִשְׁמַת אָדָם; חֹפֵשׂ, כָּל-חַדְרֵי-בָטֶן
ner hashem nishmat adam; chofes, kol-chadrei-vaten
The spirit of man is the lamp of the LORD, searching all the inward parts.

חֶסֶד וֶאֱמֶת, יִצְּרוּ-מֶלֶךְ; וְסָעַד בַּחֶסֶד כִּסְאוֹ
chesed ve'emet yitzeru-melech; vesa'ad bachesed kis'o
Mercy and truth preserve the king; and his throne is upheld by mercy.

תִּפְאֶרֶת בַּחוּרִים כֹּחָם; וַהֲדַר זְקֵנִים שֵׂיבָה
tif'eret bachurim kocham; vahadar zekenim seivah
The glory of young men is their strength; and the beauty of old men is the hoary head.

חַבֻּרוֹת פֶּצַע, תַּמְרוּק בְּרָע; וּמַכּוֹת, חַדְרֵי-בָטֶן
chabburot petza tamruk bera'; umakkot, chadrei-vaten
Sharp wounds cleanse away evil; so do stripes that reach the inward parts.

כא

פַּלְגֵי-מַיִם לֶב-מֶלֶךְ, בְּיַד-יְהוָה; עַל-כָּל-אֲשֶׁר יַחְפֹּץ יַטֶּנּוּ
Palgei-mayim lev-melech beyad-hashem al-kol-'asher yachpotz yattennu
The king's heart is in the hand of the LORD as the watercourses: He turneth it whithersoever He will.

כָּל-דֶּרֶךְ-אִישׁ, יָשָׁר בְּעֵינָיו; וְתֹכֵן לִבּוֹת יְהוָה
kol-derech-'ish yashar be'einav; vetochen libbot hashem
Every way of a man is right in his own eyes; but the LORD weigheth the hearts.

עֲשֹׂה, צְדָקָה וּמִשְׁפָּט--נִבְחָר לַיהוָה מִזָּבַח
'asoh tzedakah umishpat; nivchar lahashem mizzavach
To do righteousness and justice is more acceptable to the LORD than sacrifice.

רוּם-עֵינַיִם, וּרְחַב-לֵב--נִר רְשָׁעִים חַטָּאת
rum-'einayim urechav-lev; nir resha'im chattat
A haughty look, and a proud heart--the tillage of the wicked is sin.

אֹזֶן שֹׁמַעַת, וְעַיִן רֹאָה--יְהוָה, עָשָׂה גַּם-שְׁנֵיהֶם
'ozen shoma'at ve'ayin ro'ah; hashem asah gam-sheneihem
The hearing ear, and the seeing eye, the LORD hath made even both of them.

אַל-תֶּאֱהַב שֵׁנָה, פֶּן-תִּוָּרֵשׁ; פְּקַח עֵינֶיךָ שְׂבַע-לָחֶם
'al-te'ehav shenah pen-tivvaresh; pekach eineicha seva'-lachem
Love not sleep, lest thou come to poverty; open thine eyes, and thou shalt have bread in plenty.

רַע רַע, יֹאמַר הַקּוֹנֶה; וְאֹזֵל לוֹ, אָז יִתְהַלָּל
ra ra yomar hakkoneh; ve'ozel lo, az yit'hallal
'It is bad, it is bad', saith the buyer; but when he is gone his way, then he boasteth.

יֵשׁ זָהָב, וְרָב-פְּנִינִים; וּכְלִי יְקָר, שִׂפְתֵי-דָעַת
yesh zahav verav-peninim; ucheli yekar, siftei-da'at
There is gold, and a multitude of rubies; but the lips of knowledge are a precious jewel.

לְקַח-בִּגְדוֹ, כִּי-עָרַב זָר; וּבְעַד נָכְרִיָּה חַבְלֵהוּ
lekach-bigdo ki-'arav zar; uve'ad nocheriyah chavlehu
Take his garment that is surety for a stranger; and hold him in pledge that is surety for an alien woman.

עָרֵב לָאִישׁ, לֶחֶם שָׁקֶר; וְאַחַר, יִמָּלֵא-פִיהוּ חָצָץ
'arev la'ish lechem shaker; ve'achar, yimmale-fihu chatzatz
Bread of falsehood is sweet to a man; but afterwards his mouth shall be filled with gravel.

מַחֲשָׁבוֹת, בְּעֵצָה תִכּוֹן; וּבְתַחְבֻּלוֹת, עֲשֵׂה מִלְחָמָה
machashavot be'etzah tikkon; uvetachbulot, aseh milchamah
Every purpose is established by counsel; and with good advice carry on war.

גּוֹלֶה-סּוֹד, הוֹלֵךְ רָכִיל; וּלְפֹתֶה שְׂפָתָיו, לֹא תִתְעָרָב
goleh-sod holech rachil; ulefoteh sefatav, lo tit'arav
He that goeth about as a talebearer revealeth secrets; therefore meddle not with him that openeth wide his lips.

מְקַלֵּל, אָבִיו וְאִמּוֹ--יִדְעַךְ נֵרוֹ, בֶּאֱשׁוּן חֹשֶׁךְ
mekallel aviv ve'immo; yid'ach nero, be'eshun choshech
Whoso curseth his father or his mother, his lamp shall be put out in the blackest darkness.

נַחֲלָה, מְבֹהֶלֶת בָּרִאשׁוֹנָה; וְאַחֲרִיתָהּ, לֹא תְבֹרָךְ
nachalah mevohelet barishonah; ve'acharitah, lo tevorach
An estate may be gotten hastily at the beginning; but the end thereof shall not be blessed.

אַל-תֹּאמַר אֲשַׁלְּמָה-רָע; קַוֵּה לַיהוָה, וְיֹשַׁע לָךְ
'al-tomar ashallemah-ra'; kavveh lahashem veyosha lach
Say not thou: 'I will requite evil'; wait for the LORD, and He will save thee.

תּוֹעֲבַת יְהוָה, אֶבֶן וָאָבֶן; וּמֹאזְנֵי מִרְמָה לֹא-טוֹב
to'avat hashem even va'aven; umozenei mirmah lo-tov
Divers weights are an abomination to the LORD; and a false balance is not good.

כ

לֵץ הַיַּיִן, הֹמֶה שֵׁכָר; וְכָל-שֹׁגֶה בּוֹ, לֹא יֶחְכָּם
Letz hayain homeh shechar; vechol-shogeh bo, lo yechkam
Wine is a mocker, strong drink is riotous; and whosoever reeleth thereby is not wise.

נַהַם כַּכְּפִיר, אֵימַת מֶלֶךְ; מִתְעַבְּרוֹ, חוֹטֵא נַפְשׁוֹ
naham kakkefir eimat melech; mit'abbero, chotei nafsho
The terror of a king is as the roaring of a lion: he that provoketh him to anger forfeiteth his life.

כָּבוֹד לָאִישׁ, שֶׁבֶת מֵרִיב; וְכָל-אֱוִיל, יִתְגַּלָּע
kavod la'ish shevet meriv; vechol-'evil, yitgalla
It is an honour for a man to keep aloof from strife; but every fool will be snarling.

מֵחֹרֶף, עָצֵל לֹא-יַחֲרֹשׁ; וְשָׁאַל בַּקָּצִיר וָאָיִן
mechoref atzel lo-yacharosh; vesha'al bakkatzir va'ayin
The sluggard will not plow when winter setteth in; therefore he shall beg in harvest, and have nothing.

מַיִם עֲמֻקִּים, עֵצָה בְלֶב-אִישׁ; וְאִישׁ תְּבוּנָה יִדְלֶנָּה
mayim amukkim etzah velev-'ish; ve'ish tevunah yidlennah
Counsel in the heart of man is like deep water; but a man of understanding will draw it out.

רָב-אָדָם--יִקְרָא, אִישׁ חַסְדּוֹ; וְאִישׁ אֱמוּנִים, מִי יִמְצָא
rav-'adam, yikra ish chasdo; ve'ish emunim, mi yimtza
Most men will proclaim every one his own goodness; but a faithful man who can find?

מִתְהַלֵּךְ בְּתֻמּוֹ צַדִּיק; אַשְׁרֵי בָנָיו אַחֲרָיו
mit'hallech betummo tzaddik; ashrei vanav acharav
He that walketh in his integrity as a just man, happy are his children after him.

מֶלֶךְ, יוֹשֵׁב עַל-כִּסֵּא-דִין--מְזָרֶה בְעֵינָיו כָּל-רָע
melech, yoshev al-kisse-din; mezareh ve'einav kol-ra
A king that sitteth on the throne of judgment scattereth away all evil with his eyes.

מִי-יֹאמַר, זִכִּיתִי לִבִּי; טָהַרְתִּי, מֵחַטָּאתִי
mi-yomar zikkiti libbi; taharti, mechattati
Who can say: 'I have made my heart clean, I am pure from my sin'?

אֶבֶן וָאֶבֶן, אֵיפָה וְאֵיפָה--תּוֹעֲבַת יְהוָה, גַּם-שְׁנֵיהֶם
'even va'even eifah ve'eifah; to'avat hashem gam-sheneihem
Divers weights, and divers measures, both of them alike are an abomination to the LORD.

גַּם בְּמַעֲלָלָיו, יִתְנַכֶּר-נָעַר--אִם-זַךְ וְאִם-יָשָׁר פָּעֳלוֹ
gam bema'alalav yitnakker-na'ar; im-zach ve'im-yashar po'olo
Even a child is known by his doings, whether his work be pure, and whether it be right.

גְּדָל-חֵמָה, נֹשֵׂא עֹנֶשׁ: כִּי אִם-תַּצִּיל, וְעוֹד תּוֹסִף

gedol-chemah nosei onesh; ki im-tatzil, ve'od tosif

A man of great wrath shall suffer punishment; for if thou interpose, thou wilt add thereto.

שְׁמַע עֵצָה, וְקַבֵּל מוּסָר--לְמַעַן, תֶּחְכַּם בְּאַחֲרִיתֶךָ

shema etzah vekabbel musar; lema'an, techkam be'acharitecha

Hear counsel, and receive instruction, that thou mayest be wise in thy latter end.

רַבּוֹת מַחֲשָׁבוֹת בְּלֶב-אִישׁ; וַעֲצַת יְהוָה, הִיא תָקוּם

rabbot machashavot belev-'ish; va'atzat hashem hi takum

There are many devices in a man's heart; but the counsel of the LORD, that shall stand.

תַּאֲוַת אָדָם חַסְדּוֹ; וְטוֹב-רָשׁ, מֵאִישׁ כָּזָב

ta'avat adam chasdo; vetov-rash me'ish kazav

The lust of a man is his shame; and a poor man is better than a liar.

יִרְאַת יְהוָה לְחַיִּים; וְשָׂבֵעַ יָלִין, בַּל-יִפָּקֶד רָע

yir'at hashem lechayim; vesavea yalin, bal-yippaked ra

The fear of the LORD tendeth to life; and he that hath it shall abide satisfied, he shall not be visited with evil.

טָמַן עָצֵל יָדוֹ, בַּצַּלָּחַת; גַּם-אֶל-פִּיהוּ, לֹא יְשִׁיבֶנָּה

taman atzel yado batzallachat; gam-'el-pihu, lo yeshivennah

The sluggard burieth his hand in the dish, and will not so much as bring it back to his mouth.

לֵץ תַּכֶּה, וּפֶתִי יַעְרִם

letz takkeh ufeti ya'rim

When thou smitest a scorner, the simple will become prudent;

וְהוֹכִיחַ לְנָבוֹן, יָבִין דָּעַת

vehochiach lenavon, yavin da'at

and when one that hath understanding is reproved, he will understand knowledge.

מְשַׁדֶּד-אָב, יַבְרִיחַ אֵם--בֵּן, מֵבִישׁ וּמַחְפִּיר

meshadded-'av yavriach em; ben, mevish umachpir

A son that dealeth shamefully and reproachfully will despoil his father, and chase away his mother.

חֲדַל-בְּנִי, לִשְׁמֹעַ מוּסָר; לִשְׁגוֹת, מֵאִמְרֵי-דָעַת

chadal-beni lishmoa musar; lishgot, me'imrei-da'at

Cease, my son, to hear the instruction that causeth to err from the words of knowledge.

עֵד בְּלִיַּעַל, יָלִיץ מִשְׁפָּט; וּפִי רְשָׁעִים, יְבַלַּע-אָוֶן

'ed beliya'al yalitz mishpat; ufi resha'im, yevalla'-'aven

An ungodly witness mocketh at right; and the mouth of the wicked devoureth iniquity.

נָכוֹנוּ לַלֵּצִים שְׁפָטִים; וּמַהֲלֻמוֹת, לְגֵו כְּסִילִים

nachonu lalletzim shefatim; umahalumot, legev kesilim

Judgments are prepared for scorners, and stripes for the back of fools.

מְרַדֵּף אֲמָרִים לוֹ-הֵמָּה
meraddef amarim lo-hemmah
He that pursueth words, they turn against him.

קְנֶה-לֵּב, אֹהֵב נַפְשׁוֹ; שֹׁמֵר תְּבוּנָה, לִמְצֹא-טוֹב
koneh-lev ohev nafsho; shomer tevunah, limtzo-tov
He that getteth wisdom loveth his own soul; he that keepeth understanding shall find good.

עֵד שְׁקָרִים, לֹא יִנָּקֶה; וְיָפִיחַ כְּזָבִים יֹאבֵד
'ed shekarim lo yinnakeh; veyafiach kezavim yoved
A false witness shall not be unpunished; and he that breatheth forth lies shall perish

לֹא-נָאוֶה לִכְסִיל תַּעֲנוּג; אַף, כִּי-לְעֶבֶד מְשֹׁל בְּשָׂרִים
lo-naveh lichsil ta'anug; af, ki-le'eved meshol besarim
Luxury is not seemly for a fool; much less for a servant to have rule over princes.

שֵׂכֶל אָדָם, הֶאֱרִיךְ אַפּוֹ; וְתִפְאַרְתּוֹ, עֲבֹר עַל-פָּשַׁע
sechel adam he'erich appo; vetif'arto, avor al-pasha
It is the discretion of a man to be slow to anger, and it is his glory to pass over a transgression.

נַהַם כַּכְּפִיר, זַעַף מֶלֶךְ; וּכְטַל עַל-עֵשֶׂב רְצוֹנוֹ
naham kakkefir za'af melech; uchetal al-'esev retzono
The king's wrath is as the roaring of a lion; but his favour is as dew upon the grass.

הַוֹּת לְאָבִיו, בֵּן כְּסִיל; וְדֶלֶף טֹרֵד, מִדְיְנֵי אִשָּׁה
havvot le'aviv ben kesil; vedelef tored, midyenei ishah
A foolish son is the calamity of his father; and the contentions of a wife are a continual dropping.

בַּיִת וָהוֹן, נַחֲלַת אָבוֹת; וּמֵיְהוָה, אִשָּׁה מַשְׂכָּלֶת
bayit vahon nachalat avot; umehashem, ishah maskalet
House and riches are the inheritance of fathers; but a prudent wife is from the LORD.

עַצְלָה, תַּפִּיל תַּרְדֵּמָה; וְנֶפֶשׁ רְמִיָּה תִרְעָב
'atzlah tappil tardemah; venefesh remiyah tir'av
Slothfulness casteth into a deep sleep; and the idle soul shall suffer hunger.

שֹׁמֵר מִצְוָה, שֹׁמֵר נַפְשׁוֹ; בּוֹזֵה דְרָכָיו יָמוּת
shomer mitzvah shomer nafsho; bozeh derachav yamut
He that keepeth the commandment keepeth his soul; but he that despiseth His ways shall die.

מַלְוֵה יְהוָה, חוֹנֵן דָּל; וּגְמֻלוֹ, יְשַׁלֶּם-לוֹ
malveh hashem chonen dal; ugemulo, yeshallem-lo
He that is gracious unto the poor lendeth unto the LORD; and his good deed will He repay unto him.

יַסֵּר בִּנְךָ, כִּי-יֵשׁ תִּקְוָה; וְאֶל-הֲמִיתוֹ, אַל-תִּשָּׂא נַפְשֶׁךָ
yasser bincha ki-yesh tikvah; ve'el-hamito, al-tissa nafshecha
Chasten thy son, for there is hope; but set not thy heart on his destruction.

מָוֶת וְחַיִּים, בְּיַד-לָשׁוֹן; וְאֹהֲבֶיהָ, יֹאכַל פִּרְיָהּ
mavet vechayim beyad-lashon; ve'ohaveiha, yochal piryah
Death and life are in the power of the tongue; and they that indulge it shall eat the fruit thereof.

מָצָא אִשָּׁה, מָצָא טוֹב; וַיָּפֶק רָצוֹן, מֵיְהוָה
matza ishah matza tov; vayafek ratzon, mehashem
Whoso findeth a wife findeth a great good, and obtaineth favour of the LORD.

תַּחֲנוּנִים יְדַבֶּר-רָשׁ; וְעָשִׁיר, יַעֲנֶה עַזּוֹת
tachanunim yedabber-rash; ve'ashir, ya'aneh azzot
The poor useth entreaties; but the rich answereth impudently.

אִישׁ רֵעִים, לְהִתְרֹעֵעַ; וְיֵשׁ אֹהֵב, דָּבֵק מֵאָח
'ish re'im lehitro'ea'; veyesh ohev, davek me'ach
There are friends that one hath to his own hurt; but there is a friend that sticketh closer than a brother.

יט

טוֹב-רָשׁ, הוֹלֵךְ בְּתֻמּוֹ--מֵעִקֵּשׁ שְׂפָתָיו, וְהוּא כְסִיל
Tov-rash holech betummo; me'ikkesh sefatav, vehu chesil
Better is the poor that walketh in his integrity than he that is perverse in his lips and a fool at the same time.

גַּם בְּלֹא-דַעַת נֶפֶשׁ לֹא-טוֹב; וְאָץ בְּרַגְלַיִם חוֹטֵא
gam belo-da'at nefesh lo-tov; ve'atz beraglayim chote
Also, that the soul be without knowledge is not good; and he that hasteth with his feet sinneth.

אִוֶּלֶת אָדָם, תְּסַלֵּף דַּרְכּוֹ; וְעַל-יְהוָה, יִזְעַף לִבּוֹ
'ivvelet adom tesallef darko; ve'al-hashem yiz'af libbo
The foolishness of man perverteth his way; and his heart fretteth against the LORD.

הוֹן--יֹסִיף, רֵעִים רַבִּים; וְדָל, מֵרֵעֵהוּ יִפָּרֵד
hon, yosif re'im rabbim; vedal, mere'hu yippared
Wealth addeth many friends; but as for the poor, his friend separateth himself from him.

עֵד שְׁקָרִים, לֹא יִנָּקֶה; וְיָפִיחַ כְּזָבִים, לֹא יִמָּלֵט
'ed shekarim lo yinnakeh; veyafiach kezavim, lo yimmalet
A false witness shall not be unpunished; and he that breatheth forth lies shall not escape.

רַבִּים, יְחַלּוּ פְנֵי-נָדִיב; וְכָל-הָרֵעַ, לְאִישׁ מַתָּן
rabbim yechallu fenei-nadiv; vechol-harea', le'ish mattan
Many will entreat the favour of the liberal man; and every man is a friend to him that giveth gifts.

כָּל אֲחֵי-רָשׁ, שְׂנֵאֻהוּ--אַף כִּי מְרֵעֵהוּ, רָחֲקוּ מִמֶּנּוּ
kol achei-rash sene'uhu, af ki mere'ehu rachaku mimmennu
All the brethren of the poor do hate him; how much more do his friends go far from him!

גַּם, מִתְרַפֶּה בִמְלַאכְתּוֹ--אָח הוּא, לְבַעַל מַשְׁחִית

gam mitrappeh vimlachto; ach hu, leva'al mashchit

Even one that is slack in his work is brother to him that is a destroyer.

מִגְדַּל-עֹז, שֵׁם יְהוָה; בּוֹ-יָרוּץ צַדִּיק וְנִשְׂגָּב

migdal-'oz shem hashem bo-yarutz tzaddik venisgav

The name of the LORD is a strong tower: the righteous runneth into it, and is set up on high.

הוֹן עָשִׁיר, קִרְיַת עֻזּוֹ; וּכְחוֹמָה נִשְׂגָּבָה, בְּמַשְׂכִּתוֹ

hon ashir kiryat uzzo; uchechomah nisgavah, bemaskito

The rich man's wealth is his strong city, and as a high wall in his own conceit.

לִפְנֵי-שֶׁבֶר, יִגְבַּהּ לֵב-אִישׁ; וְלִפְנֵי כָבוֹד עֲנָוָה

lifnei-shever yigbah lev-'ish; velifnei chavod anavah

Before destruction the heart of a man is haughty, and before honour goeth humility.

מֵשִׁיב דָּבָר, בְּטֶרֶם יִשְׁמָע--אִוֶּלֶת הִיא-לוֹ, וּכְלִמָּה

meshiv davor beterem yishma'; ivvelet hi-lo, uchelimmah

He that giveth answer before he heareth, it is folly and confusion unto him.

רוּחַ-אִישׁ, יְכַלְכֵּל מַחֲלֵהוּ; וְרוּחַ נְכֵאָה, מִי יִשָּׂאֶנָּה

ruach-'ish yechalkel machalehu; veruach neche'ah, mi yissa'ennah

The spirit of a man will sustain his infirmity; but a broken spirit who can bear?

לֵב נָבוֹן, יִקְנֶה-דָּעַת; וְאֹזֶן חֲכָמִים, תְּבַקֶּשׁ-דָּעַת

lev navon yikneh-da'at; ve'ozen chachamim, tevakkesh-da'at

The heart of the prudent getteth knowledge; and the ear of the wise seeketh knowledge.

מַתָּן אָדָם, יַרְחִיב לוֹ; וְלִפְנֵי גְדֹלִים יַנְחֶנּוּ

mattan adam yarchiv lo; velifnei gedolim yanchennu

A man's gift maketh room for him, and bringeth him before great men.

צַדִּיק הָרִאשׁוֹן בְּרִיבוֹ; וּבָא-רֵעֵהוּ, וַחֲקָרוֹ

tzaddik harishon berivo; uva-re'ehu, vachakaro

He that pleadeth his cause first seemeth just; but his neighbour cometh and searcheth him out.

מִדְיָנִים, יַשְׁבִּית הַגּוֹרָל; וּבֵין עֲצוּמִים יַפְרִיד

midyanim yashbit haggoral; uvein atzumim yafrid

The lot causeth strife to cease, and parteth asunder the contentious.

אָח--נִפְשָׁע מִקִּרְיַת-עֹז; וּמִדְיָנִים, כִּבְרִיחַ אַרְמוֹן

'ach, nifsha mikkiryat-'oz; umidyanim, kivriach armon

A brother offended is harder to be won than a strong city; and their contentions are like the bars of a castle.

מִפְּרִי פִי-אִישׁ, תִּשְׂבַּע בִּטְנוֹ; תְּבוּאַת שְׂפָתָיו יִשְׂבָּע

mipperi fi-'ish tisba bitno; tevu'at sefatav yisba

A man's belly shall be filled with the fruit of his mouth; with the increase of his lips shall he be satisfied.

חוֹשֵׂךְ אֲמָרָיו, יוֹדֵעַ דָּעַת; יְקַר-רוּחַ, אִישׁ תְּבוּנָה
chosech amarav yodea da'at; yekar-ruach, ish tevunah
He that spareth his words hath knowledge; and he that husbandeth his spirit is a man of discernment.

גַּם אֱוִיל מַחֲרִישׁ, חָכָם יֵחָשֵׁב
gam evil macharish chacham yechashev
Even a fool, when he holdeth his peace, is counted wise;

אֹטֵם שְׂפָתָיו נָבוֹן
otem sefatav navon
and he that shutteth his lips is esteemed as a man of understanding.

יח

לְתַאֲוָה, יְבַקֵּשׁ נִפְרָד; בְּכָל-תּוּשִׁיָּה, יִתְגַּלָּע
Leta'avah yevakkesh nifrad; bechol-tushiyah, yitgalla
He that separateth himself seeketh his own desire, and snarlest against all sound wisdom.

לֹא-יַחְפֹּץ כְּסִיל, בִּתְבוּנָה: כִּי, אִם-בְּהִתְגַּלּוֹת לִבּוֹ
lo-yachpotz kesil bitvunah; ki, im-behitgallot libbo
A fool hath no delight in understanding, but only that his heart may lay itself bare.

בְּבוֹא-רָשָׁע, בָּא גַם-בּוּז; וְעִם-קָלוֹן חֶרְפָּה
bevo-rasha ba gam-buz; ve'im-kalon cherpah
When the wicked cometh, there cometh also contempt, and with ignominy reproach.

מַיִם עֲמֻקִּים, דִּבְרֵי פִי-אִישׁ; נַחַל נֹבֵעַ, מְקוֹר חָכְמָה
mayim amukkim divrei fi-'ish; nachal novea', mekor chochmah
The words of a man's mouth are as deep waters; a flowing brook, a fountain of wisdom.

שְׂאֵת פְּנֵי-רָשָׁע לֹא-טוֹב--לְהַטּוֹת צַדִּיק, בַּמִּשְׁפָּט
se'et penei-rasha lo-tov; lehattot tzaddik, bammishpat
It is not good to respect the person of the wicked, so as to turn aside the righteous in judgment.

שִׂפְתֵי כְסִיל, יָבֹאוּ בְרִיב; וּפִיו, לְמַהֲלֻמוֹת יִקְרָא
siftei chesil yavo'u veriv; ufiv, lemahalumot yikra
A fool's lips enter into contention, and his mouth calleth for strokes.

פִּי-כְסִיל, מְחִתָּה-לוֹ; וּשְׂפָתָיו, מוֹקֵשׁ נַפְשׁוֹ
pi-chesil mechittah-lo; usefatav, mokesh nafsho
A fool's mouth is his ruin, and his lips are the snare of his soul.

דִּבְרֵי נִרְגָּן, כְּמִתְלַהֲמִים; וְהֵם, יָרְדוּ חַדְרֵי-בָטֶן
divrei nirgon kemitlahamim; vehem, yaredu chadrei-vaten
The words of a whisperer are as dainty morsels, and they go down into the innermost parts of the belly.

מַצְדִּיק רָשָׁע, וּמַרְשִׁיעַ צַדִּיק--תּוֹעֲבַת יְהוָה, גַּם-שְׁנֵיהֶם

matzdik rasho umarshia tzaddik; to'avat hashem gam-sheneihem

He that justifieth the wicked, and he that condemneth the righteous, even they both are an abomination to the LORD.

לָמָּה-זֶּה מְחִיר בְּיַד-כְּסִיל--לִקְנוֹת חָכְמָה וְלֶב-אָיִן

lammah-zeh mechir beyad-kesil; liknot chochmah velev-'ayin

Wherefore is there a price in the hand of a fool to buy wisdom, seeing he hath no understanding?

בְּכָל-עֵת, אֹהֵב הָרֵעַ; וְאָח לְצָרָה, יִוָּלֵד

bechol-'et ohev harea'; ve'ach letzarah, yivvaled

A friend loveth at all times, and a brother is born for adversity.

אָדָם חֲסַר-לֵב, תּוֹקֵעַ כָּף; עֹרֵב עֲרֻבָּה, לִפְנֵי רֵעֵהוּ

'adam chasar-lev tokea kaf; orev arubbah, lifnei re'ehu

A man void of understanding is he that striketh hands, and becometh surety in the presence of his neighbour.

אֹהֵב פֶּשַׁע, אֹהֵב מַצָּה; מַגְבִּיהַּ פִּתְחוֹ, מְבַקֶּשׁ-שָׁבֶר

'ohev pesha ohev matzah; magbiah pitcho, mevakkesh-shaver

He loveth transgression that loveth strife; he that exalteth his gate seeketh destruction.

עִקֶּשׁ-לֵב, לֹא יִמְצָא-טוֹב; וְנֶהְפָּךְ בִּלְשׁוֹנוֹ, יִפּוֹל בְּרָעָה

'ikkesh-lev lo yimtza-tov; venehpach bilshono, yippol bera'ah

He that hath a froward heart findeth no good; and he that hath a perverse tongue falleth into evil.

יֹלֵד כְּסִיל, לְתוּגָה לוֹ; וְלֹא-יִשְׂמַח, אֲבִי נָבָל

yoled kesil letugah lo; velo-yismach, avi naval

He that begetteth a fool doeth it to his sorrow; and the father of a churl hath no joy.

לֵב שָׂמֵחַ, יֵיטִיב גֵּהָה; וְרוּחַ נְכֵאָה, תְּיַבֶּשׁ-גָּרֶם

lev sameach yeitiv gehah; veruach neche'ah, teyabbesh-garem

A merry heart is a good medicine; but a broken spirit drieth the bones.

שֹׁחַד מֵחֵק, רָשָׁע יִקָּח--לְהַטּוֹת, אָרְחוֹת מִשְׁפָּט

shochad mecheik rasha yikkach; lehattot, orechot mishpat

A wicked man taketh a gift out of the bosom, to pervert the ways of justice.

אֶת-פְּנֵי מֵבִין חָכְמָה; וְעֵינֵי כְסִיל, בִּקְצֵה-אָרֶץ

'et-penei mevin chochmah ve'einei chesil, biktzeh-'aretz

Wisdom is before him that hath understanding; but the eyes of a fool are in the ends of the earth.

כַּעַס לְאָבִיו, בֵּן כְּסִיל; וּמֶמֶר, לְיוֹלַדְתּוֹ

ka'as le'aviv ben kesil; umemer, leyoladto

A foolish son is vexation to his father, and bitterness to her that bore him.

גַּם עֲנוֹשׁ לַצַּדִּיק לֹא-טוֹב--לְהַכּוֹת נְדִיבִים עַל-יֹשֶׁר

gam anosh latzaddik lo-tov; lehakkot nedivim al-yosher

To punish also the righteous is not good, nor to strike the noble for their uprightness.

מַצְרֵף לַכֶּסֶף, וְכוּר לַזָּהָב; וּבֹחֵן לִבּוֹת יְהוָה

matzref lakkesef vechur lazzahav; uvochen libbot hashem

The refining pot is for silver, and the furnace for gold; but the LORD trieth the hearts.

מֵרַע, מַקְשִׁיב עַל-שְׂפַת-אָוֶן; שֶׁקֶר מֵזִין, עַל-לְשׁוֹן הַוֹּת

mera makshiv al-sefat-'aven; sheker mezin al-leshon havvot

A evil-doer giveth heed to wicked lips; and a liar giveth ear to a mischievous tongue.

לֹעֵג לָרָשׁ, חֵרֵף עֹשֵׂהוּ; שָׂמֵחַ לְאֵיד, לֹא יִנָּקֶה

lo'eg larosh cheref osehu; sameach le'eid, lo yinnakeh

Whoso mocketh the poor blasphemeth his Maker; and he that is glad at calamity shall not be unpunished.

עֲטֶרֶת זְקֵנִים, בְּנֵי בָנִים; וְתִפְאֶרֶת בָּנִים אֲבוֹתָם

'ateret zekenim benei vanim; vetif'eret banim avotam

Children's children are the crown of old men; and the glory of children are their fathers.

לֹא-נָאוָה לְנָבָל שְׂפַת-יֶתֶר; אַף, כִּי-לְנָדִיב שְׂפַת-שָׁקֶר

lo-navah lenaval sefat-yeter; af, ki-lenadiv sefat-shaker

Overbearing speech becometh not a churl; much less do lying lips a prince.

אֶבֶן-חֵן הַשֹּׁחַד, בְּעֵינֵי בְעָלָיו; אֶל-כָּל-אֲשֶׁר יִפְנֶה יַשְׂכִּיל

'even-chen hashochad be'einei ve'alav; el-kol-'asher yifneh yaskil

A gift is as a precious stone in the eyes of him that hath it; whithersoever he turneth, he prospereth.

מְכַסֶּה-פֶּשַׁע, מְבַקֵּשׁ אַהֲבָה; וְשֹׁנֶה בְדָבָר, מַפְרִיד אַלּוּף

mechasseh-pesha mevakkesh ahavah; veshoneh vedavar, mafrid alluf

He that covereth a transgression seeketh love; but he that harpeth on a matter estrangeth a familiar friend.

תֵּחַת גְּעָרָה בְמֵבִין--מֵהַכּוֹת כְּסִיל מֵאָה

techat ge'arah vemevin; mehakkot kesil me'ah

A rebuke entereth deeper into a man of understanding than a hundred stripes into a fool.

אַךְ-מְרִי יְבַקֶּשׁ-רָע; וּמַלְאָךְ אַכְזָרִי, יְשֻׁלַּח-בּוֹ

'ach-meri yevakkesh-ra'; umal'ach achzari, yeshullach-bo

A rebellious man seeketh only evil; therefore a cruel messenger shall be sent against him.

פָּגוֹשׁ דֹּב שַׁכּוּל בְּאִישׁ; וְאַל-כְּסִיל, בְּאִוַּלְתּוֹ

pagosh dov shakkul be'ish; ve'al-kesil, be'ivvalto

Let a bear robbed of her whelps meet a man, rather than a fool in his folly.

מֵשִׁיב רָעָה, תַּחַת טוֹבָה--לֹא-תָמוּשׁ רָעָה, מִבֵּיתוֹ

meshiv ra'ah tachat tovah; lo-tamush ra'ah, mibbeito

Whoso rewardeth evil for good, evil shall not depart from his house.

פּוֹטֵר מַיִם, רֵאשִׁית מָדוֹן; וְלִפְנֵי הִתְגַּלַּע, הָרִיב נְטוֹשׁ

poter mayim reshit madon; velifnei hitgalla', hariv netosh

The beginning of strife is as when one letteth out water; therefore leave off contention, before the quarrel break out.

נֶפֶשׁ עָמֵל, עָמְלָה לּוֹ: כִּי-אָכַף עָלָיו פִּיהוּ

nefesh amel amelah lo; ki-'achaf alav pihu

The hunger of the labouring man laboureth for him; for his mouth compelleth him.

אִישׁ בְּלִיַּעַל, כֹּרֶה רָעָה; וְעַל-שְׂפָתוֹ, כְּאֵשׁ צָרָבֶת

'ish beliya'al koreh ra'ah; ve'al-sefato, ke'esh tzaravet

An ungodly man diggeth up evil, and in his lips there is as a burning fire.

אִישׁ תַּהְפֻּכוֹת, יְשַׁלַּח מָדוֹן; וְנִרְגָּן, מַפְרִיד אַלּוּף

'ish tahpuchot yeshallach madon; venirgan, mafrid alluf

A froward man soweth strife; and a whisperer separateth familiar friends.

אִישׁ חָמָס, יְפַתֶּה רֵעֵהוּ; וְהוֹלִיכוֹ, בְּדֶרֶךְ לֹא-טוֹב

'ish chamas yefatteh re'ehu; veholicho, bederech lo-tov

A man of violence enticeth his neighbour, and leadeth him into a way that is not good.

עֹצֶה עֵינָיו, לַחְשֹׁב תַּהְפֻּכוֹת; קֹרֵץ שְׂפָתָיו, כִּלָּה רָעָה

'otzeh einav lachshov tahpuchot; koretz sefatav, killah ra'ah

He that shutteth his eyes, it is to devise froward things; he that biteth his lips bringeth evil to pass.

עֲטֶרֶת תִּפְאֶרֶת שֵׂיבָה; בְּדֶרֶךְ צְדָקָה, תִּמָּצֵא

'ateret tif'eret seivah; bederech tzedakah, timmatze

The hoary head is a crown of glory, it is found in the way of righteousness.

טוֹב אֶרֶךְ אַפַּיִם, מִגִּבּוֹר; וּמֹשֵׁל בְּרוּחוֹ, מִלֹּכֵד עִיר

tov erech appayim miggibbor; umoshel berucho, milloched ir

He that is slow to anger is better than the mighty; and he that ruleth his spirit than he that taketh a city.

בַּחֵיק, יוּטַל אֶת-הַגּוֹרָל; וּמֵיהוָה, כָּל-מִשְׁפָּטוֹ

bacheik yutal et-haggoral; umehashem, kol-mishpato

The lot is cast into the lap; but the whole disposing thereof is of the LORD.

יז

טוֹב פַּת חֲרֵבָה, וְשַׁלְוָה-בָהּ--מִבַּיִת, מָלֵא זִבְחֵי-רִיב

Tov pat charevah veshalvah-vah; mibbayit, malei zivchei-riv

Better is a dry morsel and quietness therewith, than a house full of feasting with strife.

עֶבֶד-מַשְׂכִּיל--יִמְשֹׁל, בְּבֵן מֵבִישׁ

'eved-maskil, yimshol beven mevish

A servant that dealeth wisely shall have rule over a son that dealeth shamefully,

וּבְתוֹךְ אַחִים, יַחֲלֹק נַחֲלָה

uvetoch achim, yachalok nachalah

and shall have part of the inheritance among the brethren.

חֲמַת-מֶלֶךְ מַלְאֲכֵי-מָוֶת; וְאִישׁ חָכָם יְכַפְּרֶנָּה

chamat-melech mal'achei-mavet; ve'ish chacham yechapperennah

The wrath of a king is as messengers of death; but a wise man will pacify it.

בְּאוֹר-פְּנֵי-מֶלֶךְ חַיִּים; וּרְצוֹנוֹ, כְּעָב מַלְקוֹשׁ

be'or-penei-melech chayim; uretzono, ke'av malkosh

In the light of the king's countenance is life; and his favour is as a cloud of the latter rain.

קְנֹה-חָכְמָה--מַה-טּוֹב מֵחָרוּץ; וּקְנוֹת בִּינָה, נִבְחָר מִכָּסֶף

kenoh-chochmah mah-tov mecharutz; ukenot binah, nivchar mikkasef

How much better is it to get wisdom than gold! yea, to get understanding is rather to be chosen than silver.

מְסִלַּת יְשָׁרִים, סוּר מֵרָע; שֹׁמֵר נַפְשׁוֹ, נֹצֵר דַּרְכּוֹ

mesillat yesharim sur mera'; shomer nafsho, notzer darko

The highway of the upright is to depart from evil; he that keepeth his way preserveth his soul.

לִפְנֵי-שֶׁבֶר גָּאוֹן; וְלִפְנֵי כִשָּׁלוֹן, גֹּבַהּ רוּחַ

lifnei-shever ga'on; velifnei chishalon, govah ruach

Pride goeth before destruction, and a haughty spirit before a fall.

טוֹב שְׁפַל-רוּחַ, אֶת-עֲנָוִים; מֵחַלֵּק שָׁלָל, אֶת-גֵּאִים

tov shefal-ruach et-'anavim; mechallek shalal, et-ge'im

Better it is to be of a lowly spirit with the humble, than to divide the spoil with the proud.

מַשְׂכִּיל עַל-דָּבָר, יִמְצָא-טוֹב; וּבוֹטֵחַ בַּיהוָה אַשְׁרָיו

maskil al-davor yimtza-tov; uvoteach bahashem ashrav

He that giveth heed unto the word shall find good; and whoso trusteth in the LORD, happy is he.

לַחֲכַם-לֵב, יִקָּרֵא נָבוֹן; וּמֶתֶק שְׂפָתַיִם, יֹסִיף לֶקַח

lachacham-lev yikkarei navon; umetek sefatayim, yosif lekach

The wise in heart is called a man of discernment; and the sweetness of the lips increaseth learning.

מְקוֹר חַיִּים, שֵׂכֶל בְּעָלָיו; וּמוּסַר אֱוִלִים אִוֶּלֶת

mekor chayim sechel be'alav; umusar evilim ivvelet

Understanding is a fountain of life unto him that hath it; but folly is the chastisement of fools.

לֵב חָכָם, יַשְׂכִּיל פִּיהוּ; וְעַל-שְׂפָתָיו, יֹסִיף לֶקַח

lev chacham yaskil pihu; ve'al-sefatav, yosif lekach

The heart of the wise teacheth his mouth, and addeth learning to his lips.

צוּף-דְּבַשׁ, אִמְרֵי-נֹעַם; מָתוֹק לַנֶּפֶשׁ, וּמַרְפֵּא לָעָצֶם

tzuf-devash imrei-no'am; matok lannefesh umarpei la'atzem

Pleasant words are as a honeycomb, sweet to the soul, and health to the bones.

יֵשׁ דֶּרֶךְ יָשָׁר, לִפְנֵי-אִישׁ; וְאַחֲרִיתָהּ, דַּרְכֵי-מָוֶת

yesh derech yashar lifnei-'ish; ve'acharitah, darchei-mavet

There is a way which seemeth right unto a man, but the end thereof are the ways of death.

כָּל-דַּרְכֵי-אִישׁ, זַךְ בְּעֵינָיו; וְתֹכֵן רוּחוֹת יְהוָה
kol-darchei-'ish zach be'einav; vetochen ruchot hashem
All the ways of a man are clean in his own eyes; but the LORD weigheth the spirits.

גֹּל אֶל-יְהוָה מַעֲשֶׂיךָ; וְיִכֹּנוּ, מַחְשְׁבֹתֶיךָ
gol el-hashem ma'aseicha; veyikkonu, machshevoteicha
Commit thy works unto the LORD, and thy thoughts shall be established.

כֹּל פָּעַל יְהוָה, לַמַּעֲנֵהוּ; וְגַם-רָשָׁע, לְיוֹם רָעָה
kol pa'al hashem lamma'anehu; vegam-rasha', leyom ra'ah
The LORD hath made every things for His own purpose, yea, even the wicked for the day of evil.

תּוֹעֲבַת יְהוָה, כָּל-גְּבַהּ-לֵב; יָד לְיָד, לֹא יִנָּקֶה
to'avat hashem kol-gevah-lev; yad leyad, lo yinnakeh
Every one that is proud in heart is an abomination to the LORD; my hand upon it! he shall not be unpunished.

בְּחֶסֶד וֶאֱמֶת, יְכֻפַּר עָוֹן; וּבְיִרְאַת יְהוָה, סוּר מֵרָע
bechesed ve'emet yechuppar avon; uveyir'at hashem sur mera
By mercy and truth iniquity is expiated; and by the fear of the LORD men depart from evil.

בִּרְצוֹת יְהוָה, דַּרְכֵי-אִישׁ; גַּם-אוֹיְבָיו, יַשְׁלִם אִתּוֹ
birtzot hashem darchei-'ish; gam-'oyevav, yashlim itto
When a man's ways please the LORD, He maketh even his enemies to be at peace with him.

טוֹב-מְעַט, בִּצְדָקָה--מֵרֹב תְּבוּאוֹת, בְּלֹא מִשְׁפָּט
tov-me'at bitzdakah; merov tevu'ot, belo mishpat
Better is a little with righteousness than great revenues with injustice.

לֵב אָדָם, יְחַשֵּׁב דַּרְכּוֹ; וַיהוָה, יָכִין צַעֲדוֹ
lev adam yechashev darko; vahashem, yachin tza'ado
A man's heart deviseth his way; but the LORD directeth his steps.

קֶסֶם עַל-שִׂפְתֵי-מֶלֶךְ; בְּמִשְׁפָּט, לֹא יִמְעַל-פִּיו
kesem al-siftei-melech; bemishpat, lo yim'al-piv
A divine sentence is in the lips of the king; his mouth trespasseth not in judgment.

פֶּלֶס, וּמֹאזְנֵי מִשְׁפָּט--לַיהוָה; מַעֲשֵׂהוּ, כָּל-אַבְנֵי-כִיס
peles umozenei mishpat lahashem ma'asehu, kol-'avnei-chis
A just balance and scales are the LORD'S; all the weights of the bag are His work.

תּוֹעֲבַת מְלָכִים, עֲשׂוֹת רֶשַׁע: כִּי בִצְדָקָה, יִכּוֹן כִּסֵּא
to'avat melachim asot resha'; ki vitzdakah, yikkon kisse
It is an abomination to kings to commit wickedness; for the throne is established by righteousness.

רְצוֹן מְלָכִים, שִׂפְתֵי-צֶדֶק; וְדֹבֵר יְשָׁרִים יֶאֱהָב
retzon melachim siftei-tzedek; vedover yesharim ye'ehav
Righteous lips are the delight of kings; and they love him that speaketh right.

אֹרַח חַיִּים, לְמַעְלָה לְמַשְׂכִּיל--לְמַעַן סוּר, מִשְּׁאוֹל מָטָּה
'orach chayim lema'lah lemaskil; lema'an sur, mishe'ol mattah
The path of life goeth upward for the wise, that he may depart from the nether-world beneath.

בֵּית גֵּאִים, יִסַּח יְהוָה; וְיַצֵּב, גְּבוּל אַלְמָנָה
beit ge'im yissach hashem veyatzev, gevul almanah
The LORD will pluck up the house of the proud; but He will establish the border of the widow.

תּוֹעֲבַת יְהוָה, מַחְשְׁבוֹת רָע; וּטְהֹרִים, אִמְרֵי-נֹעַם
to'avat hashem machshevot ra'; utehorim, imrei-no'am
The thoughts of wickedness are an abomination to the LORD; but words of pleasantness are pure.

עֹכֵר בֵּיתוֹ, בּוֹצֵעַ בָּצַע; וְשׂוֹנֵא מַתָּנֹת יִחְיֶה
'ocher beito botzea batza'; vesonei mattanot yichyeh
He that is greedy of gain troubleth his own house; but he that hateth gifts shall live.

לֵב צַדִּיק, יֶהְגֶּה לַעֲנוֹת; וּפִי רְשָׁעִים, יַבִּיעַ רָעוֹת
lev tzaddik yehgeh la'anot; ufi resha'im, yabbia ra'ot
The heart of the righteous studieth to answer; but the mouth of the wicked poureth out evil things.

רָחוֹק יְהוָה, מֵרְשָׁעִים; וּתְפִלַּת צַדִּיקִים יִשְׁמָע
rachok hashem meresha'im; utefillat tzaddikim yishma
The LORD is far from the wicked; but He heareth the prayer of the righteous.

מְאוֹר-עֵינַיִם, יְשַׂמַּח-לֵב; שְׁמוּעָה טוֹבָה, תְּדַשֶּׁן-עָצֶם
me'or-'einayim yesammach-lev; shemu'ah tovah, tedashen-'atzem
The light of the eyes rejoiceth the heart; and a good report maketh the bones fat.

אֹזֶן--שֹׁמַעַת, תּוֹכַחַת חַיִּים: בְּקֶרֶב חֲכָמִים תָּלִין
'ozen, shoma'at tochachat chayim; bekerev chachamim talin
The ear that hearkeneth to the reproof of life abideth among the wise.

פּוֹרֵעַ מוּסָר, מוֹאֵס נַפְשׁוֹ; וְשׁוֹמֵעַ תּוֹכַחַת, קוֹנֶה לֵּב
porea musar mo'es nafsho; veshomea tochachat, koneh lev
He that refuseth correction despiseth his own soul; but he that hearkeneth to reproof getteth understanding.

יִרְאַת יְהוָה, מוּסַר חָכְמָה; וְלִפְנֵי כָבוֹד עֲנָוָה
yir'at hashem musar chochmah velifnei chavod anavah
The fear of the LORD is the instruction of wisdom; and before honour goeth humility.

טז

לְאָדָם מַעַרְכֵי-לֵב; וּמֵיְהוָה, מַעֲנֵה לָשׁוֹן
Le'adam ma'archei-lev; umehashem, ma'aneh lashon
The preparations of the heart are man's, but the answer of the tongue is from the LORD.

לֹא יֶאֱהַב-לֵץ, הוֹכֵחַ לוֹ; אֶל-חֲכָמִים, לֹא יֵלֵךְ
lo ye'ehav-letz hocheach lo; el-chachamim, lo yelech
A scorner loveth not to be reproved; he will not go unto the wise.

לֵב שָׂמֵחַ, יֵיטִב פָּנִים; וּבְעַצְּבַת-לֵב, רוּחַ נְכֵאָה
lev sameach yeitiv panim; uve'atzevat-lev ruach neche'ah
A merry heart maketh a cheerful countenance; but by sorrow of heart the spirit is broken.

לֵב נָבוֹן, יְבַקֶּשׁ-דָּעַת; וּפִי כְסִילִים, יִרְעֶה אִוֶּלֶת
lev navon yevakkesh-da'at; ufi chesilim, yir'eh ivvelet
The heart of him that hath discernment seeketh knowledge; but the mouth of fools feedeth on folly.

כָּל-יְמֵי עָנִי רָעִים; וְטוֹב-לֵב, מִשְׁתֶּה תָמִיד
kol-yemei ani ra'im; vetov-lev, mishteh tamid
All the days of the poor are evil; but he that is of a merry heart hath a continual feast.

טוֹב-מְעַט, בְּיִרְאַת יְהוָה--מֵאוֹצָר רָב, וּמְהוּמָה בוֹ
tov-me'at beyir'at hashem me'otzar rav, umehumah vo
Better is little with the fear of the LORD, than great treasure and turmoil therewith.

טוֹב אֲרֻחַת יָרָק, וְאַהֲבָה-שָׁם--מִשּׁוֹר אָבוּס, וְשִׂנְאָה-בוֹ
tov aruchat yarak ve'ahavah-sham; mishor avus, vesin'ah-vo
Better is a dinner of herbs where love is, than a stalled ox and hatred therewith.

אִישׁ חֵמָה, יְגָרֶה מָדוֹן; וְאֶרֶךְ אַפַּיִם, יַשְׁקִיט רִיב
'ish chemah yegareh madon; ve'erech appayim, yashkit riv
A wrathful man stirreth up discord; but he that is slow to anger appeaseth strife.

דֶּרֶךְ עָצֵל, כִּמְשֻׂכַת חָדֶק; וְאֹרַח יְשָׁרִים סְלֻלָה
derech atzel kimsuchat chadek; ve'orach yesharim selulah
The way of the sluggard is as though hedged by thorns; but the path of the upright is even.

בֵּן חָכָם, יְשַׂמַּח-אָב; וּכְסִיל אָדָם, בּוֹזֶה אִמּוֹ
ben chachom yesammach-'av; uchesil adam, bozeh immo
A wise son maketh a glad father; but a foolish man despiseth his mother.

אִוֶּלֶת, שִׂמְחָה לַחֲסַר-לֵב; וְאִישׁ תְּבוּנָה, יְיַשֶּׁר-לָכֶת
'ivvelet simchah lachasar-lev; ve'ish tevunah, yeyasher-lachet
Folly is joy to him that lacketh understanding; but a man of discernment walketh straightforwards.

הָפֵר מַחֲשָׁבוֹת, בְּאֵין סוֹד; וּבְרֹב יוֹעֲצִים תָּקוּם
hafer machashavot be'ein sod; uverov yo'atzim takum
For want of counsel purposes are frustrated; but in the multitude of counsellors they are established.

שִׂמְחָה לָאִישׁ, בְּמַעֲנֵה-פִיו; וְדָבָר בְּעִתּוֹ מַה-טּוֹב
simchah la'ish bema'aneh-fiv; vedavar be'itto mah-tov
A man hath joy in the answer of his mouth; and a word in due season, how good is it!

טו

מַעֲנֶה-רַּךְ, יָשִׁיב חֵמָה; וּדְבַר-עֶצֶב, יַעֲלֶה-אָף
Ma'aneh-rach yashiv chemah; udevar-'etzev, ya'aleh-'af
A soft answer turneth away wrath; but a grievous word stirreth up anger.

לְשׁוֹן חֲכָמִים, תֵּיטִיב דָּעַת; וּפִי כְסִילִים, יַבִּיעַ אִוֶּלֶת
leshon chachamim teitiv da'at; ufi chesilim, yabbia ivvelet
The tongue of the wise useth knowledge aright; but the mouth of fools poureth out foolishness.

בְּכָל-מָקוֹם, עֵינֵי יְהוָה; צֹפוֹת, רָעִים וְטוֹבִים
bechol-makom einei hashem tzofot, ra'im vetovim
The eyes of the LORD are in every place, keeping watch upon the evil and the good.

מַרְפֵּא לָשׁוֹן, עֵץ חַיִּים; וְסֶלֶף בָּהּ, שֶׁבֶר בְּרוּחַ
marpei lashon etz chayim; veselef bah, shever beruach
A soothing tongue is a tree of life; but perverseness therein is a wound to the spirit.

אֱוִיל--יִנְאַץ, מוּסַר אָבִיו; וְשֹׁמֵר תּוֹכַחַת יַעְרִים
'evil, yin'atz musar aviv; veshomer tochachat ya'rim
A fool despiseth his father's correction; but he that regardeth reproof is prudent.

בֵּית צַדִּיק, חֹסֶן רָב; וּבִתְבוּאַת רָשָׁע נֶעְכָּרֶת
beit tzaddik chosen rav; uvitvu'at rasha ne'karet
In the house of the righteous is much treasure; but in the revenues of the wicked is trouble.

שִׂפְתֵי חֲכָמִים, יְזָרוּ דָעַת; וְלֵב כְּסִילִים לֹא-כֵן
siftei chachamim yezaru da'at; velev kesilim lo-chen
The lips of the wise disperse knowledge; but the heart of the foolish is not stedfast.

זֶבַח רְשָׁעִים, תּוֹעֲבַת יְהוָה; וּתְפִלַּת יְשָׁרִים רְצוֹנוֹ
zevach resha'im to'avat hashem utefillat yesharim retzono
The sacrifice of the wicked is an abomination to the LORD; but the prayer of the upright is His delight.

תּוֹעֲבַת יְהוָה, דֶּרֶךְ רָשָׁע; וּמְרַדֵּף צְדָקָה יֶאֱהָב
to'avat hashem derech rasha'; umeraddef tzedakah ye'ehav
The way of the wicked is an abomination to the LORD; but He loveth him that followeth after righteousness.

מוּסָר רָע, לְעֹזֵב אֹרַח; שׂוֹנֵא תוֹכַחַת יָמוּת
musar ra le'ozev orach; sonei tochachat yamut
There is grievous correction for him that forsaketh the way; and he that hateth reproof shall die.

שְׁאוֹל וַאֲבַדּוֹן, נֶגֶד יְהוָה; אַף, כִּי-לִבּוֹת בְּנֵי-אָדָם
she'ol va'avaddon neged hashem af, ki-libbot benei-'adam
The nether-world and Destruction are before the LORD; how much more then the hearts of the children of men!

עֲטֶרֶת חֲכָמִים עָשְׁרָם; אִוֶּלֶת כְּסִילִים אִוֶּלֶת

'ateret chachamim osheram; ivvelet kesilim ivvelet

The crown of the wise is their riches; but the folly of fools remaineth folly.

מַצִּיל נְפָשׁוֹת, עֵד אֱמֶת; וְיָפִחַ כְּזָבִים מִרְמָה

matzil nefashot ed emet; veyafiach kezavim mirmah

A true witness delivereth souls; but he that breatheth forth lies is all deceit.

בְּיִרְאַת יְהוָה, מִבְטַח-עֹז; וּלְבָנָיו, יִהְיֶה מַחְסֶה

beyir'at hashem mivtach-'oz; ulevanav, yihyeh machseh

In the fear of the LORD a man hath strong confidence; and his children shall have a place of refuge.

יִרְאַת יְהוָה, מְקוֹר חַיִּים--לָסוּר, מִמֹּקְשֵׁי מָוֶת

yir'at hashem mekor chayim; lasur, mimmokeshei mavet

The fear of the LORD is a fountain of life, to depart from the snares of death.

בְּרָב-עָם הַדְרַת-מֶלֶךְ; וּבְאֶפֶס לְאֹם, מְחִתַּת רָזוֹן

berav-'am hadrat-melech; uve'efes le'om, mechittat razon

In the multitude of people is the king's glory; but in the want of people is the ruin of the prince.

אֶרֶךְ אַפַּיִם, רַב-תְּבוּנָה; וּקְצַר-רוּחַ, מֵרִים אִוֶּלֶת

'erech appayim rav-tevunah; uketzar-ruach, merim ivvelet

He that is slow to anger is of great understanding; but he that is hasty of spirit exalteth folly.

חַיֵּי בְשָׂרִים, לֵב מַרְפֵּא; וּרְקַב עֲצָמוֹת קִנְאָה

chayei vesarim lev marpe; urekav atzamot kin'ah

A tranquil heart is the life of the flesh; but envy is the rottenness of the bones.

עֹשֵׁק דָּל, חֵרֵף עֹשֵׂהוּ; וּמְכַבְּדוֹ, חֹנֵן אֶבְיוֹן

'oshek-dal cheref osehu; umechabbedo, chonen evyon

He that oppresseth the poor blasphemeth his Maker; but he that is gracious unto the needy honoureth Him.

בְּרָעָתוֹ, יִדָּחֶה רָשָׁע; וְחֹסֶה בְמוֹתוֹ צַדִּיק

bera'ato yiddacheh rasha'; vechoseh vemoto tzaddik

The wicked is thrust down in his misfortune; but the righteous, even when he is brought to death, hath hope.

בְּלֵב נָבוֹן, תָּנוּחַ חָכְמָה; וּבְקֶרֶב כְּסִילִים, תִּוָּדֵעַ

belev navon tanuach chochmah uvekerev kesilim, tivvadea

In the heart of him that hath discernment wisdom resteth; but in the inward part of fools it maketh itself known.

צְדָקָה תְרוֹמֵם-גּוֹי; וְחֶסֶד לְאֻמִּים חַטָּאת

tzedakah teromem-goy; vechesed le'ummim chattat

Righteousness exalteth a nation; but sin is a reproach to any people.

רְצוֹן-מֶלֶךְ, לְעֶבֶד מַשְׂכִּיל; וְעֶבְרָתוֹ, תִּהְיֶה מֵבִישׁ

retzon-melech le'eved maskil; ve'evrato, tihyeh mevish

The king's favour is toward a servant that dealeth wisely; but his wrath striketh him that dealeth shamefully.

יֵשׁ דֶּרֶךְ יָשָׁר, לִפְנֵי-אִישׁ; וְאַחֲרִיתָהּ, דַּרְכֵי-מָוֶת

yesh derech yashar lifnei-'ish; ve'acharitah, darchei-mavet

There is a way which seemeth right unto a man, but the end thereof are the ways of death.

גַּם-בִּשְׂחֹק יִכְאַב-לֵב; וְאַחֲרִיתָהּ שִׂמְחָה תוּגָה

gam-bischok yich'av-lev; ve'acharitah simchah tugah

Even in laughter the heart acheth; and the end of mirth is heaviness.

מִדְּרָכָיו יִשְׂבַּע, סוּג לֵב; וּמֵעָלָיו, אִישׁ טוֹב

midderachav yisba sug lev; ume'alav, ish tov

The dissembler in heart shall have his fill from his own ways; and a good man shall be satisfied from himself.

פֶּתִי, יַאֲמִין לְכָל-דָּבָר; וְעָרוּם, יָבִין לַאֲשֻׁרוֹ

peti ya'amin lechol-davar; ve'arum, yavin la'ashuro

The thoughtless believeth every word; but the prudent man looketh well to his going.

חָכָם יָרֵא, וְסָר מֵרָע; וּכְסִיל, מִתְעַבֵּר וּבוֹטֵחַ

chacham yarei vesar mera'; uchesil, mit'abber uvoteach

A wise man feareth, and departeth from evil; but the fool behaveth overbearingly, and is confident.

קְצַר-אַפַּיִם, יַעֲשֶׂה אִוֶּלֶת; וְאִישׁ מְזִמּוֹת, יִשָּׂנֵא

ketzar-'appayim ya'aseh ivvelet; ve'ish mezimmot, yissane

He that is soon angry dealeth foolishly; and a man of wicked devices is hated.

נָחֲלוּ פְתָאיִם אִוֶּלֶת; וַעֲרוּמִים, יַכְתִּרוּ דָעַת

nachalu fetayim ivvelet; va'arumim, yachtiru da'at

The thoughtless come into possession of folly; but the prudent are crowned with knowledge.

שַׁחוּ רָעִים, לִפְנֵי טוֹבִים; וּרְשָׁעִים, עַל-שַׁעֲרֵי צַדִּיק

shachu ra'im lifnei tovim; uresha'im, al-sha'arei tzaddik

The evil bow before the good, and the wicked at the gates of the righteous.

גַּם-לְרֵעֵהוּ, יִשָּׂנֵא רָשׁ; וְאֹהֲבֵי עָשִׁיר רַבִּים

gam-lere'ehu yissanei rash; ve'ohavei ashir rabbim

The poor is hated even of his own neighbour; but the rich hath many friends.

בָּז-לְרֵעֵהוּ חוֹטֵא; וּמְחוֹנֵן עֲנָוִים אַשְׁרָיו

baz-lere'ehu chote; umechonen anavim ashrav

He that despiseth his neighbour sinneth; but he that is gracious unto the humble, happy is he.

הֲלוֹא-יִתְעוּ, חֹרְשֵׁי רָע; וְחֶסֶד וֶאֱמֶת, חֹרְשֵׁי טוֹב

halo-yit'u choreshei ra'; vechesed ve'emet, choreshei tov

Shall they not go astray that devise evil? But mercy and truth shall be for them that devise good.

בְּכָל-עֶצֶב, יִהְיֶה מוֹתָר; וּדְבַר-שְׂפָתַיִם, אַךְ-לְמַחְסוֹר

bechol-'etzev yihyeh motar; udevar-sefatayim, ach-lemachsor

In all labour there is profit; but the talk of the lips tendeth only to penury.

יד

חַכְמוֹת נָשִׁים, בָּנְתָה בֵיתָהּ; וְאִוֶּלֶת, בְּיָדֶיהָ תֶהֶרְסֶנּוּ
Chachmot nashim banetah veitah; ve'ivvelet, beyadeiha tehersennu
Every wise woman buildeth her house; but the foolish plucketh it down with her hands.

הוֹלֵךְ בְּיָשְׁרוֹ, יְרֵא יְהוָה; וּנְלוֹז דְּרָכָיו בּוֹזֵהוּ
holech beyoshero yerei hashem uneloz derachav bozehu
He that walketh in his uprightness feareth the LORD; but he that is perverse in his ways despiseth Him.

בְּפִי-אֱוִיל, חֹטֶר גַּאֲוָה; וְשִׂפְתֵי חֲכָמִים, תִּשְׁמוּרֵם
befi-'evil choter ga'avah; vesiftei chachamim, tishmurem
In the mouth of the foolish is a rod of pride; but the lips of the wise shall preserve them.

בְּאֵין אֲלָפִים, אֵבוּס בָּר; וְרָב-תְּבוּאוֹת, בְּכֹחַ שׁוֹר
be'ein alafim evus bar; verav-tevu'ot, bechoach shor
Where no oxen are, the crib is clean; but much increase is by the strength of the ox.

עֵד אֱמוּנִים, לֹא יְכַזֵּב; וְיָפִיחַ כְּזָבִים, עֵד שָׁקֶר
'ed emunim lo yechazzev; veyafiach kezavim, ed shaker
A faithful witness will not lie; but a false witness breatheth forth lies.

בִּקֶּשׁ-לֵץ חָכְמָה וָאָיִן; וְדַעַת לְנָבוֹן נָקָל
bikkesh-letz chochmah va'ayin; veda'at lenavon nakal
A scorner seeketh wisdom, and findeth it not; but knowledge is easy unto him that hath discernment.

לֵךְ מִנֶּגֶד, לְאִישׁ כְּסִיל; וּבַל-יָדַעְתָּ, שִׂפְתֵי-דָעַת
lech minneged le'ish kesil; uval-yada'ta, siftei-da'at
Go from the presence of a foolish man, for thou wilt not perceive the lips of knowledge.

חָכְמַת עָרוּם, הָבִין דַּרְכּוֹ; וְאִוֶּלֶת כְּסִילִים מִרְמָה
chochemat arum havin darko; ve'ivvelet kesilim mirmah
The wisdom of the prudent is to look well to his way; but the folly of fools is deceit.

אֱוִלִים, יָלִיץ אָשָׁם; וּבֵין יְשָׁרִים רָצוֹן
'evilim yalitz asham; uvein yesharim ratzon
Amends pleadeth for fools; but among the upright there is good will.

לֵב--יוֹדֵעַ, מָרַּת נַפְשׁוֹ; וּבְשִׂמְחָתוֹ, לֹא-יִתְעָרַב זָר
lev, yodea marrat nafsho; uvesimchato, lo-yit'arav zar
The heart knoweth its own bitterness; and with its joy no stranger can intermeddle.

בֵּית רְשָׁעִים, יִשָּׁמֵד; וְאֹהֶל יְשָׁרִים יַפְרִיחַ
beit resha'im yishamed; ve'ohel yesharim yafriach
The house of the wicked shall be overthrown; but the tent of the upright shall flourish.

תּוֹרַת חָכָם, מְקוֹר חַיִּים--לָסוּר, מִמֹּקְשֵׁי מָוֶת

torat chacham mekor chayim; lasur, mimmokeshei mavet

The teaching of the wise is a fountain of life, to depart from the snares of death.

שֵׂכֶל-טוֹב, יִתֶּן-חֵן; וְדֶרֶךְ בֹּגְדִים אֵיתָן

sechel-tov yitten-chen; vederech bogedim eitan

Good understanding giveth grace; but the way of the faithless is harsh.

כָּל-עָרוּם, יַעֲשֶׂה בְדָעַת; וּכְסִיל, יִפְרֹשׂ אִוֶּלֶת

kol-'arum ya'aseh veda'at; uchesil, yifros ivvelet

Every prudent man dealeth with forethought; but a fool unfoldeth folly.

מַלְאָךְ רָשָׁע, יִפֹּל בְּרָע; וְצִיר אֱמוּנִים מַרְפֵּא

mal'ach rasho yippol bera'; vetzir emunim marpe

A wicked messenger falleth into evil; but a faithful ambassador is health.

רֵישׁ וְקָלוֹן, פּוֹרֵעַ מוּסָר; וְשֹׁמֵר תּוֹכַחַת יְכֻבָּד

reish vekalon porea musar; veshomer tochachat yechubbad

Poverty and shame shall be to him that refuseth instruction; but he that regardeth reproof shall be honoured.

תַּאֲוָה נִהְיָה, תֶּעֱרַב לְנָפֶשׁ; וְתוֹעֲבַת כְּסִילִים, סוּר מֵרָע

ta'avah nihyah te'erav lenafesh; veto'avat kesilim, sur mera

The desire accomplished is sweet to the soul; and it is an abomination to fools to depart from evil.

הוֹלֵךְ אֶת-חֲכָמִים יֶחְכָּם; וְרֹעֶה כְסִילִים יֵרוֹעַ

holech et-chachamim yechkam; vero'eh chesilim yeroa

He that walketh with wise men shall be wise; but the companion of fools shall smart for it.

חַטָּאִים, תְּרַדֵּף רָעָה; וְאֶת-צַדִּיקִים, יְשַׁלֶּם-טוֹב

chatta'im teraddef ra'ah; ve'et-tzaddikim, yeshallem-tov

Evil pursueth sinners; but to the righteous good shall be repaid.

טוֹב--יַנְחִיל בְּנֵי-בָנִים; וְצָפוּן לַצַּדִּיק, חֵיל חוֹטֵא

tov, yanchil benei-vanim; vetzafun latzaddik, cheil chote

A good man leaveth an inheritance to his children's children; and the wealth of the sinner is laid up for the righteous.

רָב-אֹכֶל, נִיר רָאשִׁים; וְיֵשׁ נִסְפֶּה, בְּלֹא מִשְׁפָּט

rav-'ochel nir rashim; veyesh nispeh, belo mishpat

Much food is in the tillage of the poor; but there is that is swept away by want of righteousness.

חוֹשֵׂךְ שִׁבְטוֹ, שׂוֹנֵא בְנוֹ; וְאֹהֲבוֹ, שִׁחֲרוֹ מוּסָר

chosech shivto sonei veno; ve'ohavo, shicharo musar

He that spareth his rod hateth his son; but he that loveth him chasteneth him betimes.

צַדִּיק--אֹכֵל, לְשֹׂבַע נַפְשׁוֹ; וּבֶטֶן רְשָׁעִים תֶּחְסָר

tzaddik, ochel lesova nafsho; uveten resha'im techsar

The righteous eateth to the satisfying of his desire; but the belly of the wicked shall want.

מִפְּרִי פִי-אִישׁ, יֹאכַל טוֹב; וְנֶפֶשׁ בֹּגְדִים חָמָס
mipperi fi-'ish yochal tov; venefesh bogedim chamas
A man shall eat good from the fruit of his mouth; but the desire of the faithless is violence.

נֹצֵר פִּיו, שֹׁמֵר נַפְשׁוֹ; פֹּשֵׂק שְׂפָתָיו, מְחִתָּה-לוֹ
notzer piv shomer nafsho; posek sefatav, mechittah-lo
He that guardeth his mouth keepeth his life; but for him that openeth wide his lips there shall be ruin.

מִתְאַוָּה וָאַיִן, נַפְשׁוֹ עָצֵל; וְנֶפֶשׁ חָרֻצִים תְּדֻשָּׁן
mit'avvah va'ayin nafsho atzel; venefesh charutzim tedushan
The soul of the sluggard desireth, and hath nothing; but the soul of the diligent shall be abundantly gratified.

דְּבַר-שֶׁקֶר, יִשְׂנָא צַדִּיק; וְרָשָׁע, יַבְאִישׁ וְיַחְפִּיר
devar-sheker yisna tzaddik; verasha', yav'ish veyachpir
A righteous man hateth lying; but a wicked man behaveth vilely and shamefully.

צְדָקָה, תִּצֹּר תָּם-דָּרֶךְ; וְרִשְׁעָה, תְּסַלֵּף חַטָּאת
tzedakah titzor tam-darech; verish'ah, tesallef chattat
Righteousness guardeth him that is upright in the way; but wickedness overthroweth the sinner.

יֵשׁ מִתְעַשֵּׁר, וְאֵין כֹּל; מִתְרוֹשֵׁשׁ, וְהוֹן רָב
yesh mit'asher ve'ein kol mitroshesh, vehon rav
There is that pretendeth himself rich, yet hath nothing; there is that pretendeth himself poor, yet hath great wealth.

כֹּפֶר נֶפֶשׁ-אִישׁ עָשְׁרוֹ; וְרָשׁ, לֹא-שָׁמַע גְּעָרָה
kofer nefesh-'ish oshero; verash, lo-shama ge'arah
The ransom of a man's life are his riches; but the poor heareth no threatening.

אוֹר-צַדִּיקִים יִשְׂמָח; וְנֵר רְשָׁעִים יִדְעָךְ
'or-tzaddikim yismach; vener resha'im yid'ach
The light of the righteous rejoiceth; but the lamp of the wicked shall be put out.

רַק-בְּזָדוֹן, יִתֵּן מַצָּה; וְאֶת-נוֹעָצִים חָכְמָה
rak-bezadon yitten matzah; ve'et-no'atzim chochmah
By pride cometh only contention; but with the well-advised is wisdom.

הוֹן, מֵהֶבֶל יִמְעָט; וְקֹבֵץ עַל-יָד יַרְבֶּה
hon mehevel yim'at; vekovetz al-yad yarbeh
Wealth gotten by vanity shall be diminished; but he that gathereth little by little shall increase.

תּוֹחֶלֶת מְמֻשָּׁכָה, מַחֲלָה-לֵב; וְעֵץ חַיִּים, תַּאֲוָה בָאָה
tochelet memushachah machalah-lev; ve'etz chayim, ta'avah va'ah
Hope deferred maketh the heart sick; but desire fulfilled is a tree of life.

בָּז לְדָבָר, יֵחָבֶל לוֹ; וִירֵא מִצְוָה, הוּא יְשֻׁלָּם
baz ledavar yechavel lo; viyrei mitzvah, hu yeshullam
Whoso despiseth the word shall suffer thereby; but he that feareth the commandment shall be rewarded.

שְׂפַת-אֱמֶת, תִּכּוֹן לָעַד; וְעַד-אַרְגִּיעָה, לְשׁוֹן שָׁקֶר
sefat-'emet tikkon la'ad; ve'ad-'argi'ah, leshon shaker
The lip of truth shall be established for ever; but a lying tongue is but for a moment.

מִרְמָה, בְּלֶב-חֹרְשֵׁי רָע; וּלְיֹעֲצֵי שָׁלוֹם שִׂמְחָה
mirmah belev-choreshei ra'; uleyo'atzei shalom simchah
Deceit is in the heart of them that devise evil; but to the counsellors of peace is joy.

לֹא-יְאֻנֶּה לַצַּדִּיק כָּל-אָוֶן; וּרְשָׁעִים, מָלְאוּ רָע
lo-ye'unneh latzaddik kol-'aven; uresha'im, male'u ra
There shall no mischief befall the righteous; but the wicked are filled with evil.

תּוֹעֲבַת יְהוָה, שִׂפְתֵי-שָׁקֶר; וְעֹשֵׂי אֱמוּנָה רְצוֹנוֹ
to'avat hashem siftei-shaker; ve'osei emunah retzono
Lying lips are an abomination to the LORD; but they that deal truly are His delight.

אָדָם עָרוּם, כֹּסֶה דָּעַת; וְלֵב כְּסִילִים, יִקְרָא אִוֶּלֶת
'adam arum koseh da'at; velev kesilim, yikra ivvelet
A prudent man concealeth knowledge; but the heart of fools proclaimeth foolishness.

יַד-חָרוּצִים תִּמְשׁוֹל; וּרְמִיָּה, תִּהְיֶה לָמַס
yad-charutzim timshol; uremiyah, tihyeh lamas
The hand of the diligent shall bear rule; but the slothful shall be under tribute.

דְּאָגָה בְלֶב-אִישׁ יַשְׁחֶנָּה; וְדָבָר טוֹב יְשַׂמְּחֶנָּה
de'agah velev-'ish yashchennah; vedavar tov yesammechennah
Care in the heart of a man boweth it down; but a good word maketh it glad.

יָתֵר מֵרֵעֵהוּ צַדִּיק; וְדֶרֶךְ רְשָׁעִים תַּתְעֵם
yater mere'ehu tzaddik; vederech resha'im tat'em
The righteous is guided by his friend; but the way of the wicked leadeth them astray.

לֹא-יַחֲרֹךְ רְמִיָּה צֵידוֹ; וְהוֹן-אָדָם יָקָר חָרוּץ
lo-yacharoch remiyah tzeido; vehon-'adam yakar charutz
The slothful man shall not hunt his prey; but the precious substance of men is to be diligent.

בְּאֹרַח-צְדָקָה חַיִּים; וְדֶרֶךְ נְתִיבָה אַל-מָוֶת
be'orach-tzedakah chayim; vederech netivah al-mavet
In the way of righteousness is life, and in the pathway thereof there is no death.

יג

בֵּן חָכָם, מוּסַר אָב; וְלֵץ, לֹא-שָׁמַע גְּעָרָה
Ben chacham musar av; veletz, lo-shama ge'arah
A wise son is instructed of his father; but a scorner heareth not rebuke.

לְפִי-שִׂכְלוֹ, יְהֻלַּל-אִישׁ; וְנַעֲוֵה-לֵב, יִהְיֶה לָבוּז

lefi-sichlo yehullal-'ish; vena'aveh-lev, yihyeh lavuz

A man shall be commended according to his intelligence; but he that is of a distorted understanding shall be despised.

טוֹב נִקְלֶה, וְעֶבֶד לוֹ--מִמִּתְכַּבֵּד, וַחֲסַר-לָחֶם

tov nikleh ve'eved lo; mimmetakkabbed, vachasar-lachem

Better is he that is lightly esteemed, and hath a servant, than he that playeth the man of rank, and lacketh bread.

יוֹדֵעַ צַדִּיק, נֶפֶשׁ בְּהֶמְתּוֹ; וְרַחֲמֵי רְשָׁעִים, אַכְזָרִי

yodea tzaddik nefesh behemto; verachamei resha'im, achzari

A righteous man regardeth the life of his beast; but the tender mercies of the wicked are cruel.

עֹבֵד אַדְמָתוֹ, יִשְׂבַּע-לָחֶם; וּמְרַדֵּף רֵיקִים חֲסַר-לֵב

'oved admato yisba'-lachem; umeraddef reikim chasar-lev

He that tilleth his ground shall have plenty of bread; but he that followeth after vain things is void of understanding.

חָמַד רָשָׁע, מְצוֹד רָעִים; וְשֹׁרֶשׁ צַדִּיקִים יִתֵּן

chamad rasha metzod ra'im; veshoresh tzaddikim yitten

The wicked desireth the prey of evil men; but the root of the righteous yieldeth fruit.

בְּפֶשַׁע שְׂפָתַיִם, מוֹקֵשׁ רָע; וַיֵּצֵא מִצָּרָה צַדִּיק

befesha sefatayim mokesh ra'; vayetzei mitzarah tzaddik

In the transgression of the lips is a snare to the evil man; but the righteous cometh out of trouble.

מִפְּרִי פִי-אִישׁ, יִשְׂבַּע-טוֹב

mipperi fi-'ish yisba'-tov

A man shall be satisfied with good by the fruit of his mouth,

וּגְמוּל יְדֵי-אָדָם, יָשִׁיב לוֹ

ugemul yedei-'adam, yashiv lo

and the doings of a man's hands shall be rendered unto him.

דֶּרֶךְ אֱוִיל, יָשָׁר בְּעֵינָיו; וְשֹׁמֵעַ לְעֵצָה חָכָם

derech evil yashar be'einav; veshomea le'etzah chacham

The way of a fool is straight in his own eyes; but he that is wise hearkeneth unto counsel.

אֱוִיל--בַּיּוֹם, יִוָּדַע כַּעְסוֹ; וְכֹסֶה קָלוֹן עָרוּם

'evil, bayom yivvada ka'so; vechoseh kalon arum

A fool's vexation is presently known; but a prudent man concealeth shame.

יָפִיחַ אֱמוּנָה, יַגִּיד צֶדֶק; וְעֵד שְׁקָרִים מִרְמָה

yafiach emunah yaggid tzedek; ve'ed shekarim mirmah

He that breatheth forth truth uttereth righteousness; but a false witness deceit.

יֵשׁ בּוֹטֶה, כְּמַדְקְרוֹת חָרֶב; וּלְשׁוֹן חֲכָמִים מַרְפֵּא

yesh boteh kemadkerot charev; uleshon chachamim marpe

There is that speaketh like the piercings of a sword; but the tongue of the wise is health.

בֹּטֵחַ בְּעָשְׁרוֹ, הוּא יִפֹּל; וְכֶעָלֶה, צַדִּיקִים יִפְרָחוּ
boteach be'oshero hu yippol; veche'aleh, tzaddikim yifrachu
He that trusteth in his riches shall fall; but the righteous shall flourish as foliage.

עֹכֵר בֵּיתוֹ, יִנְחַל-רוּחַ; וְעֶבֶד אֱוִיל, לַחֲכַם-לֵב
'ocher beito yinchal-ruach; ve'eved evil, lachacham-lev
He that troubleth his own house shall inherit the wind; and the foolish shall be servant to the wise of heart.

פְּרִי-צַדִּיק, עֵץ חַיִּים; וְלֹקֵחַ נְפָשׁוֹת חָכָם
peri-tzaddik etz chayim; velokeach nefasot chacham
The fruit of the righteous is a tree of life; and he that is wise winneth souls.

הֵן צַדִּיק, בָּאָרֶץ יְשֻׁלָּם; אַף, כִּי-רָשָׁע וְחוֹטֵא
hen tzaddik ba'aretz yeshullam; af, ki-rasha vechotei
Behold, the righteous shall be requited in the earth; how much more the wicked and the sinner!

יב

אֹהֵב מוּסָר, אֹהֵב דָּעַת; וְשֹׂנֵא תוֹכַחַת בָּעַר
Ohev musar ohev da'at; vesonei tochachat ba'ar
Whoso loveth knowledge loveth correction; but he that is brutish hateth reproof.

טוֹב--יָפִיק רָצוֹן, מֵיְהוָה; וְאִישׁ מְזִמּוֹת יַרְשִׁיעַ
tov, yafik ratzon mehashem; ve'ish mezimmot yarshia
A good man shall obtain favour of the LORD; but a man of wicked devices will He condemn.

לֹא-יִכּוֹן אָדָם בְּרֶשַׁע; וְשֹׁרֶשׁ צַדִּיקִים, בַּל-יִמּוֹט
lo-yikkon adam beresha'; veshoresh tzaddikim, bal-yimmot
A man shall not be established by wickedness; but the root of the righteous shall never be moved.

אֵשֶׁת-חַיִל, עֲטֶרֶת בַּעְלָהּ; וּכְרָקָב בְּעַצְמוֹתָיו מְבִישָׁה
'eshet-chayil ateret ba'lah; ucherakav be'atzmotav mevishah
A virtuous woman is a crown to her husband; but she that doeth shamefully is as rottenness in his bones.

מַחְשְׁבוֹת צַדִּיקִים מִשְׁפָּט; תַּחְבֻּלוֹת רְשָׁעִים מִרְמָה
machshevot tzaddikim mishpat; tachbulot resha'im mirmah
The thoughts of the righteous are right; but the counsels of the wicked are deceit.

דִּבְרֵי רְשָׁעִים אֱרָב-דָּם; וּפִי יְשָׁרִים, יַצִּילֵם
divrei resha'im erov-dam; ufi yesharim, yatzilem
The words of the wicked are to lie in wait for blood; but the mouth of the upright shall deliver them.

הָפוֹךְ רְשָׁעִים וְאֵינָם; וּבֵית צַדִּיקִים יַעֲמֹד
hafoch resha'im ve'einam; uveit tzaddikim ya'amod
The wicked are overthrown, and are not; but the house of the righteous shall stand.

גֹּמֵל נַפְשׁוֹ, אִישׁ חָסֶד; וְעֹכֵר שְׁאֵרוֹ, אַכְזָרִי

gomel nafsho ish chased; ve'ocher she'ero, achzari

The merciful man doeth good to his own soul; but he that is cruel troubleth his own flesh.

רָשָׁע--עֹשֶׂה פְעֻלַּת-שָׁקֶר; וְזֹרֵעַ צְדָקָה, שֶׂכֶר אֱמֶת

rasha', oseh fe'ullat-shaker; vezorea tzedakah, secher emet

The wicked earneth deceitful wages; but he that soweth righteousness hath a sure reward.

כֵּן-צְדָקָה לְחַיִּים; וּמְרַדֵּף רָעָה לְמוֹתוֹ

ken-tzedakah lechayim; umeraddef ra'ah lemoto

Stedfast righteousness tendeth to life; but he that pursueth evil pursueth it to his own death.

תּוֹעֲבַת יְהוָה, עִקְּשֵׁי-לֵב; וּרְצוֹנוֹ, תְּמִימֵי דָרֶךְ

to'avat hashem ikkeshei-lev; uretzono, temimei darech

They that are perverse in heart are an abomination to the LORD; but such as are upright in their way are His delight.

יָד לְיָד, לֹא-יִנָּקֶה רָּע; וְזֶרַע צַדִּיקִים נִמְלָט

yad leyad lo-yinnakeh ra'; vezera tzaddikim nimlat

My hand upon it! the evil man shall not be unpunished; but the seed of the righteous shall escape.

נֶזֶם זָהָב, בְּאַף חֲזִיר--אִשָּׁה יָפָה, וְסָרַת טָעַם

nezem zahov be'af chazir; ishah yafah, vesarat ta'am

As a ring of gold in a swine's snout, so is a fair woman that turneth aside from discretion.

תַּאֲוַת צַדִּיקִים אַךְ-טוֹב; תִּקְוַת רְשָׁעִים עֶבְרָה

ta'avat tzaddikim ach-tov; tikvat resha'im evrah

The desire of the righteous is only good; but the expectation of the wicked is wrath.

יֵשׁ מְפַזֵּר, וְנוֹסָף עוֹד

yesh mefazzer venosaf od

There is that scattereth, and yet increaseth;

וְחוֹשֵׂךְ מִיֹּשֶׁר, אַךְ-לְמַחְסוֹר

vechosech miyosher, ach-lemachsor

and there is that withholdeth more than is meet, but it tendeth only to want.

נֶפֶשׁ-בְּרָכָה תְדֻשָּׁן; וּמַרְוֶה, גַּם-הוּא יוֹרֶא

nefesh-berachah tedushan; umarveh, gam-hu yore

The beneficent soul shall be made rich, and he that satisfieth abundantly shall be satisfied also himself.

מֹנֵעַ בָּר, יִקְּבֻהוּ לְאוֹם; וּבְרָכָה, לְרֹאשׁ מַשְׁבִּיר

monea bar yikkevuhu le'om; uverachah, lerosh mashbir

He that withholdeth corn, the people shall curse him; but blessing shall be upon the head of him that selleth it.

שֹׁחֵר טוֹב, יְבַקֵּשׁ רָצוֹן; וְדֹרֵשׁ רָעָה תְבוֹאֶנּוּ

shocher tov yevakkesh ratzon; vedoresh ra'ah tevo'ennu

He that diligently seeketh good seeketh favour; but he that searcheth for evil, it shall come unto him.

צִדְקַת יְשָׁרִים, תַּצִּילֵם; וּבְהַוַּת, בֹּגְדִים יִלָּכֵדוּ

tzidkat yesharim tatzilem; uvehavvat, bogedim yillachedu

The righteousness of the upright shall deliver them; but the faithless shall be trapped in their own crafty device.

בְּמוֹת אָדָם רָשָׁע, תֹּאבַד תִּקְוָה; וְתוֹחֶלֶת אוֹנִים אָבָדָה

bemot adam rasha tovad tikvah; vetochelet onim avadah

When a wicked man dieth, his expectation shall perish, and the hope of strength perisheth.

צַדִּיק, מִצָּרָה נֶחֱלָץ; וַיָּבֹא רָשָׁע תַּחְתָּיו

tzaddik mitzarah nechelatz; vayavo rasha tachtav

The righteous is delivered out of trouble, and the wicked cometh in his stead.

בְּפֶה--חָנֵף, יַשְׁחִת רֵעֵהוּ

befeh, chanef yashchit re'ehu

With his mouth the impious man destroyeth his neighbour;

וּבְדַעַת, צַדִּיקִים יֵחָלֵצוּ

uveda'at, tzaddikim yechaletzu

but through knowledge shall the righteous be delivered.

בְּטוּב צַדִּיקִים, תַּעֲלֹץ קִרְיָה; וּבַאֲבֹד רְשָׁעִים רִנָּה

betuv tzaddikim ta'alotz kiryah; uva'avod resha'im rinnah

When it goeth well with the righteous, the city rejoiceth; and when the wicked perish, there is joy.

בְּבִרְכַּת יְשָׁרִים, תָּרוּם קָרֶת; וּבְפִי רְשָׁעִים, תֵּהָרֵס

bevirkat yesharim tarum karet; uvefi resha'im, tehares

By the blessing of the upright a city is exalted; but it is overthrown by the mouth of the wicked.

בָּז-לְרֵעֵהוּ חֲסַר-לֵב; וְאִישׁ תְּבוּנוֹת יַחֲרִישׁ

baz-lere'ehu chasar-lev; ve'ish tevunot yacharish

He that despiseth his neighbour lacketh understanding; but a man of discernment holdeth his peace.

הוֹלֵךְ רָכִיל, מְגַלֶּה-סּוֹד; וְנֶאֱמַן-רוּחַ, מְכַסֶּה דָבָר

holech rachil megalleh-sod; vene'eman-ruach, mechasseh davar

He that goeth about as a talebearer revealeth secrets; but he that is of a faithful spirit concealeth a matter.

בְּאֵין תַּחְבֻּלוֹת, יִפָּל-עָם; וּתְשׁוּעָה, בְּרֹב יוֹעֵץ

be'ein tachbulot yippol-'am; utshu'ah, berov yo'etz

Where no wise direction is, a people falleth; but in the multitude of counsellors there is safety.

רַע-יֵרוֹעַ, כִּי-עָרַב זָר; וְשֹׂנֵא תֹקְעִים בּוֹטֵחַ

ra'-yeroa ki-'arav zar; vesonei toke'im boteach

He that is surety for a stranger shall smart for it; but he that hateth them that strike hands is secure.

אֵשֶׁת-חֵן, תִּתְמֹךְ כָּבוֹד; וְעָרִיצִים, יִתְמְכוּ-עֹשֶׁר

'eshet-chen titmoch kavod; ve'aritzim, yitmechu-'osher

A gracious woman obtaineth honour; and strong men obtain riches.

יְרְאַת יְהוָה, תּוֹסִיף יָמִים; וּשְׁנוֹת רְשָׁעִים תִּקְצֹרְנָה
yir'at hashem tosif yamim; ushenot resha'im tiktzorenah
The fear of the LORD prolongeth days; but the years of the wicked shall be shortened.

תּוֹחֶלֶת צַדִּיקִים שִׂמְחָה; וְתִקְוַת רְשָׁעִים תֹּאבֵד
tochelet tzaddikim simchah; vetikvat resha'im toved
The hope of the righteous is gladness; but the expectation of the wicked shall perish.

מָעוֹז לַתֹּם, דֶּרֶךְ יְהוָה; וּמְחִתָּה, לְפֹעֲלֵי אָוֶן
ma'oz lattom derech hashem umechittah, lefo'alei aven
The way of the LORD is a stronghold to the upright, but ruin to the workers of iniquity.

צַדִּיק, לְעוֹלָם בַּל-יִמּוֹט; וּרְשָׁעִים, לֹא יִשְׁכְּנוּ-אָרֶץ
tzaddik le'olam bal-yimmot; uresha'im, lo yishkenu-'aretz
The righteous shall never be moved; but the wicked shall not inhabit the land.

פִּי-צַדִּיק, יָנוּב חָכְמָה; וּלְשׁוֹן תַּהְפֻּכוֹת, תִּכָּרֵת
pi-tzaddik yanuv chochmah uleshon tahpuchot, tikkaret
The mouth of the righteous buddeth with wisdom; but the froward tongue shall be cut off.

שִׂפְתֵי צַדִּיק, יֵדְעוּן רָצוֹן; וּפִי רְשָׁעִים, תַּהְפֻּכוֹת
siftei tzaddik yede'un ratzon; ufi resha'im, tahpuchot
The lips of the righteous know what is acceptable; but the mouth of the wicked is all frowardness.

יא

מֹאזְנֵי מִרְמָה, תּוֹעֲבַת יְהוָה; וְאֶבֶן שְׁלֵמָה רְצוֹנוֹ
Mozenei mirmah to'avat hashem ve'even shelemah retzono
A false balance is an abomination to the LORD; but a perfect weight is His delight.

בָּא-זָדוֹן, וַיָּבֹא קָלוֹן; וְאֶת-צְנוּעִים חָכְמָה
ba-zadon vayavo kalon; ve'et-tzenu'im chochmah
When pride cometh, then cometh shame; but with the lowly is wisdom.

תֻּמַּת יְשָׁרִים תַּנְחֵם; וְסֶלֶף בֹּגְדִים יְשָׁדֵּם
tummat yesharim tanchem; veselef bogedim yeshaddem
The integrity of the upright shall guide them; but the perverseness of the faithless shall destroy them.

לֹא-יוֹעִיל הוֹן, בְּיוֹם עֶבְרָה; וּצְדָקָה, תַּצִּיל מִמָּוֶת
lo-yo'il hon beyom evrah; utzedakah, tatzil mimmavet
Riches profit not in the day of wrath; but righteousness delivereth from death.

צִדְקַת תָּמִים, תְּיַשֵּׁר דַּרְכּוֹ; וּבְרִשְׁעָתוֹ, יִפֹּל רָשָׁע
tzidkat tamim teyasher darko; uverish'ato, yippol rasha
The righteousness of the sincere shall make straight his way; but the wicked shall fall by his own wickedness.

הוֹן עָשִׁיר, קִרְיַת עֻזּוֹ; מְחִתַּת דַּלִּים רֵישָׁם
hon ashir kiryat uzzo; mechittat dallim reisham
The rich man's wealth is his strong city; the ruin of the poor is their poverty.

פְּעֻלַּת צַדִּיק לְחַיִּים; תְּבוּאַת רָשָׁע לְחַטָּאת
pe'ullat tzaddik lechayim; tevu'at rasha lechattat
The wages of the righteous is life; the increase of the wicked is sin.

אֹרַח לְחַיִּים, שׁוֹמֵר מוּסָר; וְעוֹזֵב תּוֹכַחַת מַתְעֶה
'orach lechayim shomer musar; ve'ozev tochachat mat'eh
He is in the way of life that heedeth instruction; but he that forsaketh reproof erreth.

מְכַסֶּה שִׂנְאָה, שִׂפְתֵי-שָׁקֶר; וּמוֹצִא דִבָּה, הוּא כְסִיל
mechasseh sin'ah siftei-shaker; umotzi dibbah, hu chesil
He that hideth hatred is of lying lips; and he that uttereth a slander is a fool.

בְּרֹב דְּבָרִים, לֹא יֶחְדַּל-פָּשַׁע; וְחֹשֵׂךְ שְׂפָתָיו מַשְׂכִּיל
berov devarim lo yechdal-pasha'; vechosech sefatav maskil
In the multitude of words there wanteth not transgression; but he that refraineth his lips is wise.

כֶּסֶף נִבְחָר, לְשׁוֹן צַדִּיק; לֵב רְשָׁעִים כִּמְעָט
kesef nivchor leshon tzaddik; lev resha'im kim'at
The tongue of the righteous is as choice silver; the heart of the wicked is little worth.

שִׂפְתֵי צַדִּיק, יִרְעוּ רַבִּים; וֶאֱוִילִים, בַּחֲסַר-לֵב יָמוּתוּ
siftei tzaddik yir'u rabbim; ve'evilim, bachasar-lev yamutu
The lips of the righteous feed many; but the foolish die for want of understanding.

בִּרְכַּת יְהוָה, הִיא תַעֲשִׁיר; וְלֹא-יוֹסִף עֶצֶב עִמָּהּ
birkat hashem hi ta'ashir; velo-yosif etzev immah
The blessing of the LORD, it maketh rich, and toil addeth nothing thereto.

כִּשְׂחוֹק לִכְסִיל, עֲשׂוֹת זִמָּה; וְחָכְמָה, לְאִישׁ תְּבוּנָה
kischok lichsil asot zimmah; vechochemah, le'ish tevunah
It is as sport to a fool to do wickedness, and so is wisdom to a man of discernment.

מְגוֹרַת רָשָׁע, הִיא תְבוֹאֶנּוּ; וְתַאֲוַת צַדִּיקִים יִתֵּן
megorat rasho hi tevo'ennu; veta'avat tzaddikim yitten
The fear of the wicked, it shall come upon him; and the desire of the righteous shall be granted.

כַּעֲבוֹר סוּפָה, וְאֵין רָשָׁע; וְצַדִּיק, יְסוֹד עוֹלָם
ka'avor sufah ve'ein rasha'; vetzaddik, yesod olam
When the whirlwind passeth, the wicked is no more; but the righteous is an everlasting foundation.

כַּחֹמֶץ, לַשִּׁנַּיִם--וְכֶעָשָׁן לָעֵינָיִם: כֵּן הֶעָצֵל, לְשֹׁלְחָיו
kachometz lashinnayim, veche'ashan la'einayim; ken he'atzel, lesholechav
As vinegar to the teeth, and as smoke to the eyes, so is the sluggard to them that send him.

רֹאשׁ--עֹשֶׂה כַף-רְמִיָּה; וְיַד חָרוּצִים תַּעֲשִׁיר
rash, oseh chaf-remiyah; veyad charutzim ta'ashir
He becometh poor that dealeth with a slack hand; but the hand of the diligent maketh rich.

אֹגֵר בַּקַּיִץ, בֵּן מַשְׂכִּיל; נִרְדָּם בַּקָּצִיר, בֵּן מֵבִישׁ
'oger bakkayitz ben maskil; nirdam bakkatzir, ben mevish
A wise son gathereth in summer; but a son that doeth shamefully sleepeth in harvest.

בְּרָכוֹת, לְרֹאשׁ צַדִּיק; וּפִי רְשָׁעִים, יְכַסֶּה חָמָס
berachot lerosh tzaddik; ufi resha'im, yechasseh chamas
Blessings are upon the head of the righteous; but the mouth of the wicked concealeth violence.

זֵכֶר צַדִּיק, לִבְרָכָה; וְשֵׁם רְשָׁעִים יִרְקָב
zecher tzaddik livrachah; veshem resha'im yirkav
The memory of the righteous shall be for a blessing; but the name of the wicked shall rot.

חֲכַם-לֵב, יִקַּח מִצְוֺת; וֶאֱוִיל שְׂפָתַיִם, יִלָּבֵט
chacham-lev yikkach mitzvot; ve'evil sefatayim, yillavet
The wise in heart will receive commandments; but a prating fool shall fall.

הוֹלֵךְ בַּתֹּם, יֵלֶךְ בֶּטַח; וּמְעַקֵּשׁ דְּרָכָיו, יִוָּדֵעַ
holech battom yelech betach; ume'akkesh derachav, yivvadea
He that walketh uprightly walketh securely; but he that perverteth his ways shall be found out.

קֹרֵץ עַיִן, יִתֵּן עַצָּבֶת; וֶאֱוִיל שְׂפָתַיִם, יִלָּבֵט
koretz ayin yitten atzavet; ve'evil sefatayim, yillavet
He that winketh with the eye causeth sorrow; and a prating fool shall fall.

מְקוֹר חַיִּים, פִּי צַדִּיק; וּפִי רְשָׁעִים, יְכַסֶּה חָמָס
mekor chayim pi tzaddik; ufi resha'im, yechasseh chamas
The mouth of the righteous is a fountain of life; but the mouth of the wicked concealeth violence.

שִׂנְאָה, תְּעֹרֵר מְדָנִים; וְעַל כָּל-פְּשָׁעִים, תְּכַסֶּה אַהֲבָה
sin'ah te'orer medanim; ve'al kol-pesha'im, techasseh ahavah
Hatred stirreth up strifes; but love covereth all transgressions.

בְּשִׂפְתֵי נָבוֹן, תִּמָּצֵא חָכְמָה
besiftei navon timmatzei chochmah
In the lips of him that hath discernment wisdom is found;

וְשֵׁבֶט, לְגֵו חֲסַר-לֵב
veshevet, legev chasar-lev
but a rod is for the back of him that is void of understanding.

חֲכָמִים יִצְפְּנוּ-דָעַת; וּפִי-אֱוִיל, מְחִתָּה קְרֹבָה
chachamim yitzpenu-da'at; ufi-'evil mechittah kerovah
Wise men lay up knowledge; but the mouth of the foolish is an imminent ruin.

כִּי-בִי, יִרְבּוּ יָמֶיךָ; וְיוֹסִיפוּ לְךָ, שְׁנוֹת חַיִּים
ki-vi yirbu yameicha; veyosifu lecha, shenot chayim
For by me thy days shall be multiplied, and the years of thy life shall be increased.

אִם-חָכַמְתָּ, חָכַמְתָּ לָךְ; וְלַצְתָּ, לְבַדְּךָ תִשָּׂא
'im-chachamta chachamta lach; velatzta, levaddecha tissa
If thou art wise, thou art wise for thyself; and if thou scornest, thou alone shalt bear it.'

אֵשֶׁת כְּסִילוּת, הֹמִיָּה; פְּתַיּוּת, וּבַל-יָדְעָה מָּה
'eshet kesilut homiyah; petayut, uval-yade'ah mah
The woman Folly is riotous; she is thoughtless, and knoweth nothing.

וְיָשְׁבָה, לְפֶתַח בֵּיתָהּ--עַל-כִּסֵּא, מְרֹמֵי קָרֶת
veyashevah lefetach beitah; al-kissa, meromei karet
And she sitteth at the door of her house, on a seat in the high places of the city,

לִקְרֹא לְעֹבְרֵי-דָרֶךְ; הַמְיַשְּׁרִים, אֹרְחוֹתָם
likro le'overei-darech; hamyasherim, orechotam
To call to them that pass by, who go right on their ways:

מִי-פֶתִי, יָסֻר הֵנָּה; וַחֲסַר-לֵב, וְאָמְרָה לּוֹ
mi-feti yasur hennah; vachasar-lev, ve'amerah lo
'Whoso is thoughtless, let him turn in hither'; and as for him that lacketh understanding, she saith to him:

מַיִם-גְּנוּבִים יִמְתָּקוּ; וְלֶחֶם סְתָרִים יִנְעָם
mayim-genuvim yimtaku; velechem setarim yin'am
'Stolen waters are sweet, and bread eaten in secret is pleasant.'

וְלֹא-יָדַע, כִּי-רְפָאִים שָׁם; בְּעִמְקֵי שְׁאוֹל קְרֻאֶיהָ
velo-yada ki-refa'im sham; be'imkei she'ol keru'eiha
But he knoweth not that the shades are there; that her guests are in the depths of the nether-world.

▌

מִשְׁלֵי, שְׁלֹמֹה: בֵּן חָכָם, יְשַׂמַּח-אָב; וּבֵן כְּסִיל, תּוּגַת אִמּוֹ
Mishlei, shelomoh ben chacham yesammach-'av; uven kesil, tugat immo
The proverbs of Solomon. A wise son maketh a glad father; but a foolish son is the grief of his mother.

לֹא-יוֹעִילוּ, אוֹצְרוֹת רֶשַׁע; וּצְדָקָה, תַּצִּיל מִמָּוֶת
lo-yo'ilu otzerot resha'; utzedakah, tatzil mimmavet
Treasures of wickedness profit nothing; but righteousness delivereth from death.

לֹא-יַרְעִיב יְהוָה, נֶפֶשׁ צַדִּיק; וְהַוַּת רְשָׁעִים יֶהְדֹּף
lo-yar'iv hashem nefesh tzaddik; vehavvat resha'im yehdof
The LORD will not suffer the soul of the righteous to famish; but He thrusteth away the desire of the wicked.

ט

חָכְמוֹת, בָּנְתָה בֵיתָהּ; חָצְבָה עַמּוּדֶיהָ שִׁבְעָה
Chachemot banetah veitah; chatzevah ammudeiha shiv'ah
Wisdom hath builded her house, she hath hewn out her seven pillars;

טָבְחָה טִבְחָהּ, מָסְכָה יֵינָהּ; אַף, עָרְכָה שֻׁלְחָנָהּ
tavechah tivchah masechah yeinah; af, arechah shulchanah
She hath prepared her meat, she hath mingled her wine; she hath also furnished her table.

שָׁלְחָה נַעֲרֹתֶיהָ תִקְרָא--עַל-גַּפֵּי, מְרֹמֵי קָרֶת
shalechah na'aroteiha tikra; al-gappei, meromei karet
She hath sent forth her maidens, she calleth, upon the highest places of the city:

מִי-פֶתִי, יָסֻר הֵנָּה; חֲסַר-לֵב, אָמְרָה לּוֹ
mi-feti yasur hennah; chasar-lev, amerah lo
'Whoso is thoughtless, let him turn in hither'; as for him that lacketh understanding, she saith to him:

לְכוּ, לַחֲמוּ בְלַחֲמִי; וּשְׁתוּ, בְּיַיִן מָסָכְתִּי
lechu lachamu velachami; ushetu, beyayin masacheti
'Come, eat of my bread, and drink of the wine which I have mingled.

עִזְבוּ פְתָאיִם וִחְיוּ; וְאִשְׁרוּ, בְּדֶרֶךְ בִּינָה
'izvu fetayim vichyu; ve'ishru, bederech binah
Forsake all thoughtlessness, and live; and walk in the way of understanding.

יֹסֵר, לֵץ--לֹקֵחַ לוֹ קָלוֹן
yoser letz, lokeach lo kalon
He that correcteth a scorner getteth to himself shame,

וּמוֹכִיחַ לְרָשָׁע מוּמוֹ
umochiach lerasha mumo
and he that reproveth a wicked man, it becometh unto him a blot.

אַל-תּוֹכַח לֵץ, פֶּן-יִשְׂנָאֶךָּ; הוֹכַח לְחָכָם, וְיֶאֱהָבֶךָּ
'al-tochach letz pen-yisna'eka; hochach lechacham, veye'ehaveka
Reprove not a scorner, lest he hate thee; reprove a wise man, and he will love thee.

תֵּן לְחָכָם, וְיֶחְכַּם-עוֹד; הוֹדַע לְצַדִּיק, וְיוֹסֶף לֶקַח
ten lechacham veyechkam-'od; hoda letzaddik, veyosef lekach
Give to a wise man, and he will be yet wiser; teach a righteous man, and he will increase in learning.

תְּחִלַּת חָכְמָה, יִרְאַת יְהוָה; וְדַעַת קְדֹשִׁים בִּינָה
techillat chochmah yir'at hashem veda'at kedoshim binah
The fear of the LORD is the beginning of wisdom, and the knowledge of the All-holy is understanding.

עַד-לֹא עָשָׂה, אֶרֶץ וְחוּצוֹת; וְרֹאשׁ, עַפְרוֹת תֵּבֵל

'ad-lo asah eretz vechutzot; verosh, aferot tevel

While as yet He had not made the earth, nor the fields, nor the beginning of the dust of the world.

בַּהֲכִינוֹ שָׁמַיִם, שָׁם אָנִי; בְּחֻקוֹ חוּג, עַל-פְּנֵי תְהוֹם

bahachino shamayim sham ani; bechuko chug, al-penei tehom

When He established the heavens, I was there; when He set a circle upon the face of the deep,

בְּאַמְּצוֹ שְׁחָקִים מִמַּעַל; בַּעֲזוֹז, עִינוֹת תְּהוֹם

be'ammetzo shechakim mimma'al; ba'azoz, inot tehom

When He made firm the skies above, when the fountains of the deep showed their might,

בְּשׂוּמוֹ לַיָּם, חֻקוֹ, וּמַיִם, לֹא יַעַבְרוּ-פִיו

besumo layam chukko, umayim lo ya'avru-fiv

When He gave to the sea His decree, that the waters should not transgress His commandment,

בְּחוּקוֹ, מוֹסְדֵי אָרֶץ

bechuko, mosedei aretz

when He appointed the foundations of the earth;

וָאֶהְיֶה אֶצְלוֹ, אָמוֹן: וָאֶהְיֶה שַׁעֲשׁוּעִים, יוֹם יוֹם; מְשַׂחֶקֶת לְפָנָיו בְּכָל-עֵת

va'ehyeh etzlo, amon va'ehyeh sha'ashu'im yom yom; mesacheket lefanav bechol-'et

Then I was by Him, as a nursling; and I was daily all delight, playing always before Him,

מְשַׂחֶקֶת, בְּתֵבֵל אַרְצוֹ; וְשַׁעֲשֻׁעַי, אֶת-בְּנֵי אָדָם

mesacheket betevel artzo; vesha'ashu'ai, et-benei adam

Playing in His habitable earth, and my delights are with the sons of men.

וְעַתָּה בָנִים, שִׁמְעוּ-לִי; וְאַשְׁרֵי, דְּרָכַי יִשְׁמֹרוּ

ve'attah vanim shim'u-li; ve'ashrei, derachai yishmoru

Now therefore, ye children, hearken unto me; for happy are they that keep my ways.

שִׁמְעוּ מוּסָר וַחֲכָמוּ; וְאַל-תִּפְרָעוּ

shim'u musar vachachamu, ve'al-tifra'u

Hear instruction, and be wise, and refuse it not.

אַשְׁרֵי אָדָם, שֹׁמֵעַ-לִי: לִשְׁקֹד עַל-דַּלְתֹתַי, יוֹם יוֹם--לִשְׁמֹר, מְזוּזֹת פְּתָחָי

'ashrei adam shomea li lishkod al-daltotai yom yom; lishmor, mezuzot petachai

Happy is the man that hearkeneth to me, watching daily at my gates, waiting at the posts of my doors.

כִּי מֹצְאִי, מָצָא חַיִּים; וַיָּפֶק רָצוֹן, מֵיְהוָה

ki motze'i matza chayim; vayafek ratzon, mehashem

For whoso findeth me findeth life, and obtaineth favour of the LORD.

וְחֹטְאִי, חֹמֵס נַפְשׁוֹ; כָּל-מְשַׂנְאַי, אָהֲבוּ מָוֶת

vechot'i chomes nafsho; kol-mesan'ai, ahavu mavet

But he that misseth me wrongeth his own soul; all they that hate me love death.'

לִי-עֵצָה, וְתוּשִׁיָּה; אֲנִי בִינָה, לִי גְבוּרָה
li-'etzah vetushiyah; ani vinah, li gevurah
Counsel is mine, and sound wisdom; I am understanding, power is mine.

בִּי, מְלָכִים יִמְלֹכוּ; וְרֹזְנִים, יְחֹקְקוּ צֶדֶק
bi melachim yimlochu; verozenim, yechokeku tzedek
By me kings reign, and princes decree justice.

בִּי, שָׂרִים יָשֹׂרוּ; וּנְדִיבִים, כָּל-שֹׁפְטֵי צֶדֶק
bi sarim yasoru; unedivim, kol-shofetei tzedek
By me princes rule, and nobles, even all the judges of the earth.

אֲנִי, אֹהֲבַי אֵהָב; וּמְשַׁחֲרַי, יִמְצָאֻנְנִי
'ani ohavai ehav; umeshacharai, yimtza'uneni
I love them that love me, and those that seek me earnestly shall find me.

עֹשֶׁר-וְכָבוֹד אִתִּי; הוֹן עָתֵק, וּצְדָקָה
'osher-vechavod itti; hon atek, utzedakah
Riches and honour are with me; yea, enduring riches and righteousness.

טוֹב פִּרְיִי, מֵחָרוּץ וּמִפָּז; וּתְבוּאָתִי, מִכֶּסֶף נִבְחָר
tov piryi mecharutz umippaz; utevu'ati, mikkesef nivchar
My fruit is better than gold, yea, than fine gold; and my produce than choice silver.

בְּאֹרַח-צְדָקָה אֲהַלֵּךְ; בְּתוֹךְ, נְתִיבוֹת מִשְׁפָּט
be'orach-tzedakah ahallech; betoch, netivot mishpat
I walk in the way of righteousness, in the midst of the paths of justice;

לְהַנְחִיל אֹהֲבַי יֵשׁ; וְאֹצְרֹתֵיהֶם אֲמַלֵּא
lehanchil ohavai yesh; ve'otzeroteihem amalle
That I may cause those that love me to inherit substance, and that I may fill their treasuries.

יְהוָה--קָנָנִי, רֵאשִׁית דַּרְכּוֹ: קֶדֶם מִפְעָלָיו מֵאָז
hashem kanani reshit darko; kedem mif'alav me'az
The LORD made me as the beginning of His way, the first of His works of old.

מֵעוֹלָם, נִסַּכְתִּי מֵרֹאשׁ--מִקַּדְמֵי-אָרֶץ
me'olam nissachti merosh, mikkadmei-'aretz
I was set up from everlasting, from the beginning, or ever the earth was.

בְּאֵין-תְּהֹמוֹת חוֹלָלְתִּי; בְּאֵין מַעְיָנוֹת, נִכְבַּדֵּי-מָיִם
be'ein-tehomot cholaleti; be'ein ma'yanot, nichbaddei-mayim
When there were no depths, I was brought forth; when there were no fountains abounding with water.

בְּטֶרֶם הָרִים הָטְבָּעוּ; לִפְנֵי גְבָעוֹת חוֹלָלְתִּי
beterem harim hoteba'u; lifnei geva'ot cholaleti
Before the mountains were settled, before the hills was I brought forth;

בְּרֹאשׁ-מְרֹמִים עֲלֵי-דָרֶךְ; בֵּית נְתִיבוֹת נִצָּבָה
berosh-meromim alei-darech; beit netivot nitzavah
In the top of high places by the way, where the paths meet, she standeth;

לְיַד-שְׁעָרִים לְפִי-קָרֶת; מְבוֹא פְתָחִים תָּרֹנָּה
leyad-she'arim lefi-karet; mevo fetachim taronnah
Beside the gates, at the entry of the city, at the coming in at the doors, she crieth aloud:

אֲלֵיכֶם אִישִׁים אֶקְרָא; וְקוֹלִי, אֶל-בְּנֵי אָדָם
'aleichem ishim ekra; vekoli, el-benei adam
'Unto you, O men, I call, and my voice is to the sons of men.

הָבִינוּ פְתָאיִם עָרְמָה; וּכְסִילִים, הָבִינוּ לֵב
havinu fetayim aremah; uchesilim, havinu lev
O ye thoughtless, understand prudence, and, ye fools, be ye of an understanding heart.

שִׁמְעוּ, כִּי-נְגִידִים אֲדַבֵּר; וּמִפְתַּח שְׂפָתַי, מֵישָׁרִים
shim'u ki-negidim adabber; umiftach sefatai, meisharim
Hear, for I will speak excellent things, and the opening of my lips shall be right things.

כִּי-אֱמֶת, יֶהְגֶּה חִכִּי; וְתוֹעֲבַת שְׂפָתַי רֶשַׁע
ki-'emet yehgeh chikki; veto'avat sefatai resha
For my mouth shall utter truth, and wickedness is an abomination to my lips.

בְּצֶדֶק כָּל-אִמְרֵי-פִי: אֵין בָּהֶם, נִפְתָּל וְעִקֵּשׁ
betzedek kol-'imrei-fi; ein bahem, niftal ve'ikkesh
All the words of my mouth are in righteousness, there is nothing perverse or crooked in them.

כֻּלָּם נְכֹחִים, לַמֵּבִין; וִישָׁרִים, לְמֹצְאֵי דָעַת
kullam nechochim lammevin; viysharim, lemotze'ei da'at
They are all plain to him that understandeth, and right to them that find knowledge.

קְחוּ-מוּסָרִי וְאַל-כָּסֶף; וְדַעַת, מֵחָרוּץ נִבְחָר
kechu-musari ve'al-kasef; veda'at, mecharutz nivchar
Receive my instruction, and not silver, and knowledge rather than choice gold.

כִּי-טוֹבָה חָכְמָה, מִפְּנִינִים; וְכָל-חֲפָצִים, לֹא יִשְׁווּ-בָהּ
ki-tovah chochmah mippeninim; vechol-chafatzim, lo yishvu-vah
For wisdom is better than rubies, and all things desirable are not to be compared unto her.

אֲנִי-חָכְמָה, שָׁכַנְתִּי עָרְמָה; וְדַעַת מְזִמּוֹת אֶמְצָא
'ani-chochmah shachanti oremah; veda'at mezimmot emtza
I wisdom dwell with prudence, and find out knowledge of devices.

יִרְאַת יְהוָה, שְׂנֹאת-רָע: גֵּאָה וְגָאוֹן וְדֶרֶךְ רָע, וּפִי תַהְפֻּכוֹת שָׂנֵאתִי.
yir'at hashem senot ra ge'ah vega'on vederech ra ufi tahpuchot saneti
The fear of the LORD is to hate evil; pride, and arrogancy, and the evil way, and the froward mouth, do I hate.

לְכָה נִרְוֶה דֹדִים, עַד-הַבֹּקֶר; נִתְעַלְּסָה, בָּאֲהָבִים

lechah nirveh dodim ad-habboker; nit'allesah, bo'ohavim

Come, let us take our fill of love until the morning; let us solace ourselves with loves.

כִּי אֵין הָאִישׁ בְּבֵיתוֹ; הָלַךְ, בְּדֶרֶךְ מֵרָחוֹק

ki ein ha'ish beveito; halach, bederech merachok

For my husband is not at home, he is gone a long journey;

צְרוֹר-הַכֶּסֶף, לָקַח בְּיָדוֹ; לְיוֹם הַכֶּסֶא, יָבֹא בֵיתוֹ

tzeror-hakkesef lakach beyado; leyom hakkese, yavo veito

He hath taken the bag of money with him; he will come home at the full moon.'

הִטַּתּוּ, בְּרֹב לִקְחָהּ; בְּחֵלֶק שְׂפָתֶיהָ, תַּדִּיחֶנּוּ

hittattu berov likchah; bechelek sefateiha, taddichennu

With her much fair speech she causeth him to yield, with the blandishment of her lips she enticeth him away.

הוֹלֵךְ אַחֲרֶיהָ, פִּתְאֹם: כְּשׁוֹר, אֶל-טֶבַח יָבֹא; וּכְעֶכֶס, אֶל-מוּסַר אֱוִיל

holech achareiha, pit'om keshor el-tavach yavo; uche'eches, el-musar evil

He goeth after her straightway, as an ox that goeth to the slaughter, or as one in fetters to the correction of the fool;

עַד יְפַלַּח חֵץ, כְּבֵדוֹ--כְּמַהֵר צִפּוֹר אֶל-פָּח; וְלֹא-יָדַע, כִּי-בְנַפְשׁוֹ הוּא.

'ad yefallach chetz kevedo, kemaher tzippor el-pach; velo-yada', ki-venafsho hu

Till an arrow strike through his liver; as a bird hasteneth to the snare--and knoweth not that it is at the cost of his life.

וְעַתָּה בָנִים, שִׁמְעוּ-לִי; וְהַקְשִׁיבוּ, לְאִמְרֵי-פִי

ve'attah vanim shim'u-li; vehakshivu, le'imrei-fi

Now therefore, O ye children, hearken unto me, and attend to the words of my mouth.

אַל-יֵשְׂטְ אֶל-דְּרָכֶיהָ לִבֶּךָ; אַל-תֵּתַע, בִּנְתִיבוֹתֶיהָ

'al-yest el-deracheiha libbecha; al-teta bintivoteiha

Let not thy heart decline to her ways, go not astray in her paths.

כִּי-רַבִּים חֲלָלִים הִפִּילָה; וַעֲצֻמִים, כָּל-הֲרֻגֶיהָ

ki-rabbim chalalim hippilah; va'atzumim, kol-harugeiha

For she hath cast down many wounded; yea, a mighty host are all her slain.

דַּרְכֵי שְׁאוֹל בֵּיתָהּ; יֹרְדוֹת, אֶל-חַדְרֵי-מָוֶת

darchei she'ol beitah; yoredot, el-chadrei-mavet

Her house is the way to the nether-world, going down to the chambers of death.

ח

הֲלֹא-חָכְמָה תִקְרָא; וּתְבוּנָה, תִּתֵּן קוֹלָהּ

Halo-chochmah tikra; utevunah, titten kolah

Doth not wisdom call, and understanding put forth her voice?

כִּי, בְּחַלּוֹן בֵּיתִי--בְּעַד אֶשְׁנַבִּי נִשְׁקָפְתִּי

ki bechallon beiti; be'ad eshnabbi nishkafeti

For at the window of my house I looked forth through my lattice;

וָאֵרֶא בַפְּתָאיִם, אָבִינָה בַבָּנִים--נַעַר חֲסַר-לֵב

va'erei vappetayim, avinah vabbanim, na'ar chasar-lev

And I beheld among the thoughtless ones, I discerned among the youths, a young man void of understanding,

עֹבֵר בַּשּׁוּק, אֵצֶל פִּנָּהּ; וְדֶרֶךְ בֵּיתָהּ יִצְעָד

'over bashuk etzel pinnah; vederech beitah yitz'ad

Passing through the street near her corner, and he went the way to her house;

בְּנֶשֶׁף-בְּעֶרֶב יוֹם; בְּאִישׁוֹן לַיְלָה, וַאֲפֵלָה

beneshef-be'erev yom; be'ishon laylah, va'afelah

In the twilight, in the evening of the day, in the blackness of night and the darkness.

וְהִנֵּה אִשָּׁה, לִקְרָאתוֹ; שִׁית זוֹנָה, וּנְצֻרַת לֵב

vehinneh ishah likrato; shit zonah, unetzurat lev

And, behold, there met him a woman with the attire of a harlot, and wily of heart.

הֹמִיָּה הִיא וְסֹרָרֶת; בְּבֵיתָהּ, לֹא-יִשְׁכְּנוּ רַגְלֶיהָ

homiyah hi vesoraret; beveitah, lo-yishkenu ragleiha

She is riotous and rebellious, her feet abide not in her house;

פַּעַם, בַּחוּץ--פַּעַם בָּרְחֹבוֹת; וְאֵצֶל כָּל-פִּנָּה תֶאֱרֹב

pa'am bachutz, pa'am barechovot; ve'etzel kol-pinnah te'erov

Now she is in the streets, now in the broad places, and lieth in wait at every corner.

וְהֶחֱזִיקָה בּוֹ, וְנָשְׁקָה לּוֹ; הֵעֵזָה פָנֶיהָ, וַתֹּאמַר לוֹ

vehechezikah bo venashekah-lo; he'ezah faneiha, vattomar lo

So she caught him, and kissed him, and with an impudent face she said unto him:

זִבְחֵי שְׁלָמִים עָלָי; הַיּוֹם, שִׁלַּמְתִּי נְדָרָי

zivchei shelamim alai; hayom, shillamti nedarai

'Sacrifices of peace-offerings were due from me; this day have I paid my vows.

עַל-כֵּן, יָצָאתִי לִקְרָאתֶךָ; לְשַׁחֵר פָּנֶיךָ, וָאֶמְצָאֶךָּ

'al-ken yatzati likratecha; leshacher paneicha, va'emtza'eka

Therefore came I forth to meet thee, to seek thy face, and I have found thee.

מַרְבַדִּים, רָבַדְתִּי עַרְשִׂי; חֲטֻבוֹת, אֵטוּן מִצְרָיִם

marvaddim ravadti arsi; chatuvot, etun mitzrayim

I have decked my couch with coverlets, with striped cloths of the yarn of Egypt.

נַפְתִּי מִשְׁכָּבִי--מֹר אֲהָלִים, וְקִנָּמוֹן

nafti mishkavi; mor ahalim, vekinnamon

I have perfumed my bed with myrrh, aloes, and cinnamon.

לֹא-יָבוּזוּ לַגַּנָּב, כִּי יִגְנוֹב--לְמַלֵּא נַפְשׁוֹ, כִּי יִרְעָב

lo-yavuzu laggannov ki yignov; lemallei nafsho, ki yir'av

Men do not despise a thief, if he steal to satisfy his soul when he is hungry;

וְנִמְצָא, יְשַׁלֵּם שִׁבְעָתָיִם: אֶת-כָּל-הוֹן בֵּיתוֹ יִתֵּן

venimtza yeshallem shiv'atayim; et-kol-hon beito yitten

But if he be found, he must restore sevenfold, he must give all the substance of his house.

נֹאֵף אִשָּׁה חֲסַר-לֵב; מַשְׁחִית נַפְשׁוֹ, הוּא יַעֲשֶׂנָּה

no'ef ishah chasar-lev; mashchit nafsho, hu ya'asennah

He that committeth adultery with a woman lacketh understanding; he doeth it that would destroy his own soul.

נֶגַע-וְקָלוֹן יִמְצָא; וְחֶרְפָּתוֹ, לֹא תִמָּחֶה

nega'-vekalon yimtza; vecherpato, lo timmacheh

Wounds and dishonour shall he get, and his reproach shall not be wiped away.

כִּי-קִנְאָה חֲמַת-גָּבֶר; וְלֹא-יַחְמוֹל, בְּיוֹם נָקָם

ki-kin'ah chamat-gaver; velo-yachmol, beyom nakam

For jealousy is the rage of a man, and he will not spare in the day of vengeance.

לֹא-יִשָּׂא, פְּנֵי כָל-כֹּפֶר; וְלֹא-יֹאבֶה, כִּי תַרְבֶּה-שֹׁחַד

lo-yissa penei chol-kofer; velo-yoveh, ki tarbeh-shochad

He will not regard any ransom; neither will he rest content, though thou givest many gifts.

ז

בְּנִי, שְׁמֹר אֲמָרָי; וּמִצְוֺתַי, תִּצְפֹּן אִתָּךְ

Beni shemor amarai; umitzvotai, titzpon ittach

My son, keep my words, and lay up my commandments with thee.

שְׁמֹר מִצְוֺתַי וֶחְיֵה; וְתוֹרָתִי, כְּאִישׁוֹן עֵינֶיךָ

shemor mitzvotai vechyeh; vetorati, ke'ishon eineicha

Keep my commandments and live, and my teaching as the apple of thine eye.

קָשְׁרֵם עַל-אֶצְבְּעֹתֶיךָ; כָּתְבֵם, עַל-לוּחַ לִבֶּךָ

kosherem al-'etzbe'oteicha; kotevem, al-luach libbecha

Bind them upon thy fingers, write them upon the table of thy heart.

אֱמֹר לַחָכְמָה, אֲחֹתִי אָתְּ; וּמֹדָע, לַבִּינָה תִקְרָא

'emor lachochmah achoti at; umoda', labbinah tikra

Say unto wisdom: 'Thou art my sister', and call understanding thy kinswoman;

לִשְׁמָרְךָ, מֵאִשָּׁה זָרָה; מִנָּכְרִיָּה, אֲמָרֶיהָ הֶחֱלִיקָה

lishmarecha me'ishah zarah; minnocheriyah, amareiha hechelikah

That they may keep thee from the strange woman, from the alien woman that maketh smooth her words.

יָפִיחַ כְּזָבִים, עֵד שָׁקֶר; וּמְשַׁלֵּחַ מְדָנִים, בֵּין אַחִים

yafiach kezavim ed shaker; umeshalleach medanim, bein achim

A false witness that breatheth out lies, and he that soweth discord among brethren.

נְצֹר בְּנִי, מִצְוַת אָבִיךָ; וְאַל-תִּטֹּשׁ, תּוֹרַת אִמֶּךָ

netzor beni mitzvat avicha; ve'al-tittosh, torat immecha

My son, keep the commandment of thy father, and forsake not the teaching of thy mother;

קָשְׁרֵם עַל-לִבְּךָ תָמִיד; עָנְדֵם, עַל-גַּרְגְּרֹתֶךָ

kosherem al-libbecha tamid; ondem, al-gargerotecha

Bind them continually upon thy heart, tie them about thy neck.

בְּהִתְהַלֶּכְךָ, תַּנְחֶה אֹתָךְ--בְּשָׁכְבְּךָ, תִּשְׁמֹר עָלֶיךָ

behit'hallechcha tancheh otach, beshachebecha tishmor aleicha

When thou walkest, it shall lead thee, when thou liest down, it shall watch over thee;

וַהֲקִיצוֹתָ, הִיא תְשִׂיחֶךָ

vahakitzota, hi tesichecha

and when thou awakest, it shall talk with thee.

כִּי נֵר מִצְוָה, וְתוֹרָה אוֹר; וְדֶרֶךְ חַיִּים, תּוֹכְחוֹת מוּסָר

ki ner mitzvah vetorah or; vederech chayim, tochechot musar

For the commandment is a lamp, and the teaching is light, and reproofs of instruction are the way of life;

לִשְׁמָרְךָ, מֵאֵשֶׁת רָע; מֵחֶלְקַת, לָשׁוֹן נָכְרִיָּה

lishmorecha me'eshet ra'; mechelkat, lashon nocheriyah

To keep thee from the evil woman, from the smoothness of the alien tongue.

אַל-תַּחְמֹד יָפְיָהּ, בִּלְבָבֶךָ; וְאַל-תִּקָּחֲךָ, בְּעַפְעַפֶּיהָ

'al-tachmod yafeyah bilvavecha; ve'al-tikkachacha, be'af'appeiha

Lust not after her beauty in thy heart; neither let her captivate thee with her eyelids.

כִּי בְעַד-אִשָּׁה זוֹנָה, עַד-כִּכַּר-לָחֶם: וְאֵשֶׁת אִישׁ--נֶפֶשׁ יְקָרָה תָצוּד

ki ve'ad-'ishah zonah, ad-kikkar lachem ve'eshet ish; nefesh yekarah tatzud

For on account of a harlot a man is brought to a loaf of bread, but the adulteress hunteth for the precious life.

הֲיַחְתֶּה אִישׁ אֵשׁ בְּחֵיקוֹ; וּבְגָדָיו, לֹא תִשָּׂרַפְנָה

hayachteh ish esh becheiko; uvegadav, lo tissarafnah

Can a man take fire in his bosom, and his clothes not be burned?

אִם-יְהַלֵּךְ אִישׁ, עַל-הַגֶּחָלִים; וְרַגְלָיו, לֹא תִכָּוֶינָה

'im-yehallech ish al-haggechalim; veraglav, lo tikkaveinah

Or can one walk upon hot coals, and his feet not be scorched?

כֵּן--הַבָּא, אֶל-אֵשֶׁת רֵעֵהוּ: לֹא-יִנָּקֶה, כָּל-הַנֹּגֵעַ בָּהּ

ken, habba el-'eshet re'ehu; lo yinnakeh, kol-hannogea bah

So he that goeth in to his neighbour's wife; whosoever toucheth her shall not go unpunished.

אֲשֶׁר אֵין-לָהּ קָצִין--שֹׁטֵר וּמֹשֵׁל

'asher ein-lah katzin, shoter umoshel

Which having no chief, overseer, or ruler,

תָּכִין בַּקַּיִץ לַחְמָהּ; אָגְרָה בַקָּצִיר, מַאֲכָלָהּ

tachin bakkayitz lachmah; agerah vakkatzir, ma'achalah

Provideth her bread in the summer, and gatherest her food in the harvest.

עַד-מָתַי עָצֵל תִּשְׁכָּב; מָתַי, תָּקוּם מִשְּׁנָתֶךָ

'ad-matai atzel tishkav; matai, takum mishenatecha

How long wilt thou sleep, O sluggard? When wilt thou arise out of thy sleep?

מְעַט שֵׁנוֹת, מְעַט תְּנוּמוֹת; מְעַט, חִבֻּק יָדַיִם לִשְׁכָּב

me'at shenot me'at tenumot; me'at chibbuk yadayim lishkav

'Yet a little sleep, a little slumber, a little folding of the hands to sleep'--

וּבָא-כִמְהַלֵּךְ רֵאשֶׁךָ; וּמַחְסֹרְךָ, כְּאִישׁ מָגֵן

uva-chimhallech reshecha; umachsorecha, ke'ish magen

So shall thy poverty come as a runner, and thy want as an armed man.

אָדָם בְּלִיַּעַל, אִישׁ אָוֶן; הוֹלֵךְ, עִקְּשׁוּת פֶּה

'adam beliya'al ish aven; holech, ikkeshut peh

A base person, a man of iniquity, is he that walketh with a froward mouth;

קֹרֵץ בְּעֵינָו, מֹלֵל בְּרַגְלָו; מֹרֶה, בְּאֶצְבְּעֹתָיו

koretz be'einav molel beraglav; moreh, be'etzbe'otav

That winketh with his eyes, that scrapeth with his feet, that pointeth with his fingers;

תַּהְפֻּכוֹת, בְּלִבּוֹ--חֹרֵשׁ רָע בְּכָל-עֵת; מדיָנִים יְשַׁלֵּחַ

tahpuchot belibbo, choresh ra bechol-'et; midyanim yeshalleach

Frowardness is in his heart, he deviseth evil continually; he soweth discord.

עַל-כֵּן--פִּתְאֹם, יָבוֹא אֵידוֹ; פֶּתַע יִשָּׁבֵר, וְאֵין מַרְפֵּא

'al-ken, pit'om yavo eido; peta yishaver, ve'ein marpe

Therefore shall his calamity come suddenly; on a sudden shall he be broken, and that without remedy

שֶׁשׁ-הֵנָּה, שָׂנֵא יְהוָה; וְשֶׁבַע, תּוֹעֲבַת נַפְשׁוֹ

shesh-hennah sanei hashem vesheva', to'avat nafsho

There are six things which the LORD hateth, yea, seven which are an abomination unto Him:

עֵינַיִם רָמוֹת, לְשׁוֹן שָׁקֶר; וְיָדַיִם, שֹׁפְכוֹת דָּם-נָקִי

'einayim ramot leshon shaker; veyadayim, shofechot dam-naki

Haughty eyes, a lying tongue, and hands that shed innocent blood;

לֵב--חֹרֵשׁ, מַחְשְׁבוֹת אָוֶן; רַגְלַיִם מְמַהֲרוֹת, לָרוּץ לָרָעָה

lev, choresh machshevot aven; raglayim memaharot, larutz lara'ah

A heart that deviseth wicked thoughts, feet that are swift in running to evil;

וְלָמָּה תִשְׁגֶּה בְנִי בְזָרָה; וּתְחַבֵּק, חֵק נָכְרִיָּה
velammah tishgeh veni vezarah; utechabbek, chek nacheriyah
Why then wilt thou, my son, be ravished with a strange woman, and embrace the bosom of an alien?

כִּי נֹכַח, עֵינֵי יְהוָה--דַּרְכֵי-אִישׁ; וְכָל-מַעְגְּלֹתָיו מְפַלֵּס
ki nochach einei hashem darchei-'ish; vechol-ma'gelotav mefalles
For the ways of man are before the eyes of the LORD, and He maketh even all his paths.

עֲווֹנֹתָיו--יִלְכְּדֻנוֹ אֶת-הָרָשָׁע; וּבְחַבְלֵי חַטָּאתוֹ, יִתָּמֵךְ
'avonotav, yilkeduno et-harasha'; uvechavlei chattato, yittamech
His own iniquities shall ensnare the wicked, and he shall be holden with the cords of his sin.

הוּא--יָמוּת, בְּאֵין מוּסָר; וּבְרֹב אִוַּלְתּוֹ יִשְׁגֶּה
hu, yamut be'ein musar; uverov ivvalto yishgeh
He shall die for lack of instruction; and in the greatness of his folly he shall reel.

I

בְּנִי, אִם-עָרַבְתָּ לְרֵעֶךָ; תָּקַעְתָּ לַזָּר כַּפֶּיךָ
Beni im-'aravta lere'echa; taka'ta lazzar kappeicha
My son, if thou art become surety for thy neighbour, if thou hast struck thy hands for a stranger--

נוֹקַשְׁתָּ בְאִמְרֵי-פִיךָ; נִלְכַּדְתָּ, בְּאִמְרֵי-פִיךָ
nokashta ve'imrei-ficha; nilkadta, be'imrei-ficha
Thou art snared by the words of thy mouth, thou art caught by the words of thy mouth--

עֲשֵׂה זֹאת אֵפוֹא בְּנִי, וְהִנָּצֵל--כִּי בָאתָ בְכַף-רֵעֶךָ
'aseh zot efo beni vehinnatzel, ki vata vechaf-re'echa
Do this now, my son, and deliver thyself, seeing thou art come into the hand of thy neighbour;

לֵךְ הִתְרַפֵּס, וּרְהַב רֵעֶיךָ
lech hitrappes, urehav re'eicha
go, humble thyself, and urge thy neighbour.

אַל-תִּתֵּן שֵׁנָה לְעֵינֶיךָ; וּתְנוּמָה, לְעַפְעַפֶּיךָ
'al-titten shenah le'eineicha; utenumah, le'af'appeicha
Give not sleep to thine eyes, nor slumber to thine eyelids.

הִנָּצֵל, כִּצְבִי מִיָּד; וּכְצִפּוֹר, מִיַּד יָקוּשׁ
hinnatzel kitzvi miyad; uchetzippor, miyad yakush
Deliver thyself as a gazelle from the hand [of the hunter], and as a bird from the hand of the fowler.

לֵךְ-אֶל-נְמָלָה עָצֵל; רְאֵה דְרָכֶיהָ וַחֲכָם
lech-'el-nemalah atzel; re'eh deracheiha vachacham
Go to the ant, thou sluggard; consider her ways, and be wise;

הַרְחֵק מֵעָלֶיהָ דַרְכֶּךָ; וְאַל-תִּקְרַב, אֶל-פֶּתַח בֵּיתָהּ

harchek me'aleiha darkecha; ve'al-tikrav, el-petach beitah

Remove thy way far from her, and come not nigh the door of her house;

פֶּן-תִּתֵּן לַאֲחֵרִים הוֹדֶךָ; וּשְׁנֹתֶיךָ, לְאַכְזָרִי

pen-titten la'acherim hodecha; ushenoteicha, le'achzari

Lest thou give thy vigour unto others, and thy years unto the cruel;

פֶּן-יִשְׂבְּעוּ זָרִים כֹּחֶךָ; וַעֲצָבֶיךָ, בְּבֵית נָכְרִי

pen-yisbe'u zarim kochecha; va'atzaveicha, beveit nacheri

Lest strangers be filled with thy strength, and thy labours be in the house of an alien;

וְנָהַמְתָּ בְאַחֲרִיתֶךָ; בִּכְלוֹת בְּשָׂרְךָ, וּשְׁאֵרֶךָ

venahamta ve'acharitecha; bichlot besarecha, ushe'erecha

And thou moan, when thine end cometh, when thy flesh and thy body are consumed,

וְאָמַרְתָּ--אֵיךְ, שָׂנֵאתִי מוּסָר; וְתוֹכַחַת, נָאַץ לִבִּי

ve'amarta, eich saneti musar; vetochachat, na'atz libbi

And say: 'How have I hated instruction, and my heart despised reproof;

וְלֹא-שָׁמַעְתִּי, בְּקוֹל מוֹרָי; וְלִמְלַמְּדַי, לֹא-הִטִּיתִי אָזְנִי

velo-shama'ti bekol morai; velimlammedai, lo-hittiti ozeni

Neither have I hearkened to the voice of my teachers, nor inclined mine ear to them that instructed me!

כִּמְעַט, הָיִיתִי בְכָל-רָע--בְּתוֹךְ קָהָל וְעֵדָה

kim'at hayiti vechal-ra'; betoch kahal ve'edah

I was well nigh in all evil in the midst of the congregation and assembly.'

שְׁתֵה-מַיִם מִבּוֹרֶךָ; וְנֹזְלִים, מִתּוֹךְ בְּאֵרֶךָ

sheteh-mayim mibborecha; venozelim, mittoch be'erecha

Drink waters out of thine own cistern, and running waters out of thine own well.

יָפוּצוּ מַעְיְנֹתֶיךָ חוּצָה; בָּרְחֹבוֹת, פַּלְגֵי-מָיִם

yafutzu ma'yenoteicha chutzah; barechovot, palgei-mayim

Let thy springs be dispersed abroad, and courses of water in the streets.

יִהְיוּ-לְךָ לְבַדֶּךָ; וְאֵין לְזָרִים אִתָּךְ

yihyu-lecha levaddecha; ve'ein lezarim ittach

Let them be only thine own, and not strangers' with thee.

יְהִי-מְקוֹרְךָ בָרוּךְ; וּשְׂמַח, מֵאֵשֶׁת נְעוּרֶךָ

yehi-mekorecha varuch; usemach, me'eshet ne'urecha

Let thy fountain be blessed; and have joy of the wife of thy youth.

אַיֶּלֶת אֲהָבִים, וְיַעֲלַת-חֵן: דַּדֶּיהָ, יְרַוֻּךָ בְכָל-עֵת; בְּאַהֲבָתָהּ, תִּשְׁגֶּה תָמִיד

'ayelet ahavim, veya'alat-chen daddeiha yeravvucha vechol-'et; be'ahavatah, tishgeh tamid

A lovely hind and a graceful doe, let her breasts satisfy thee at all times; with her love be thou ravished always.

הָסֵר מִמְּךָ, עִקְּשׁוּת פֶּה; וּלְזוּת שְׂפָתַיִם, הַרְחֵק מִמֶּךָּ

haser mimmecha ikkeshut peh; ulezut sefatayim, harchek mimmeka

Put away from thee a froward mouth, and perverse lips put far from thee.

עֵינֶיךָ, לְנֹכַח יַבִּיטוּ; וְעַפְעַפֶּיךָ, יַיְשִׁרוּ נֶגְדֶּךָ

'eineicha lenochach yabbitu; ve'af'appeicha, yayshiru negdecha

Let thine eyes look right on, and let thine eyelids look straight before thee.

פַּלֵּס, מַעְגַּל רַגְלֶךָ; וְכָל-דְּרָכֶיךָ יִכֹּנוּ

palles ma'gal raglecha; vechol-deracheicha yikkonu

Make plain the path of thy feet, and let all thy ways be established.

אַל-תֵּט-יָמִין וּשְׂמֹאול; הָסֵר רַגְלְךָ מֵרָע

'al-tet-yamin usmol; haser raglecha mera

Turn not to the right hand nor to the left; remove thy foot from evil.

ה

בְּנִי, לְחָכְמָתִי הַקְשִׁיבָה; לִתְבוּנָתִי, הַט-אָזְנֶךָ

Beni lechochemati hakshivah; litvunati, hat-'azenecha

My son, attend unto my wisdom; incline thine ear to my understanding;

לִשְׁמֹר מְזִמּוֹת; וְדַעַת, שְׂפָתֶיךָ יִנְצֹרוּ

lishmor mezimmot; veda'at, sefateicha yintzoru

That thou mayest preserve discretion, and that thy lips may keep knowledge.

כִּי נֹפֶת תִּטֹּפְנָה, שִׂפְתֵי זָרָה; וְחָלָק מִשֶּׁמֶן חִכָּהּ

ki nofet tittofenah siftei zarah; vechalak mishemen chikkah

For the lips of a strange woman drop honey, and her mouth is smoother than oil;

וְאַחֲרִיתָהּ, מָרָה כַלַּעֲנָה; חַדָּה, כְּחֶרֶב פִּיּוֹת

ve'acharitah marah challa'anah; chaddah, kecherev piyot

But her end is bitter as wormwood, sharp as a two-edged sword.

רַגְלֶיהָ, יֹרְדוֹת מָוֶת; שְׁאוֹל, צְעָדֶיהָ יִתְמֹכוּ

ragleiha yoredot mavet; she'ol, tze'adeiha yitmochu

Her feet go down to death; her steps take hold on the nether-world;

אֹרַח חַיִּים, פֶּן-תְּפַלֵּס; נָעוּ מַעְגְּלֹתֶיהָ, לֹא תֵדָע

'orach chayim pen-tefalles; na'u ma'geloteiha, lo teda

Lest she should walk the even path of life, her ways wander, but she knoweth it not.

וְעַתָּה בָנִים, שִׁמְעוּ-לִי; וְאַל-תָּסוּרוּ, מֵאִמְרֵי-פִי

ve'attah vanim shim'u-li; ve'al-tasuru, me'imrei-fi

Now therefore, O ye children, hearken unto me, and depart not from the words of my mouth.

בְּלֶכְתְּךָ, לֹא-יֵצַר צַעֲדֶךָ; וְאִם-תָּרוּץ, לֹא תִכָּשֵׁל
belechtecha lo-yetzar tza'adecha; ve'im-tarutz, lo tikkashel
When thou goest, thy step shall not be straitened; and if thou runnest, thou shalt not stumble.

הַחֲזֵק בַּמּוּסָר אַל-תֶּרֶף; נִצְּרֶהָ, כִּי-הִיא חַיֶּיךָ
hachazek bammusar al-teref; nitzereha, ki-hi chayeicha
Take fast hold of instruction, let her not go; keep her, for she is thy life.

בְּאֹרַח רְשָׁעִים, אַל-תָּבֹא; וְאַל-תְּאַשֵּׁר, בְּדֶרֶךְ רָעִים
be'orach resha'im al-tavo; ve'al-te'asher, bederech ra'im
Enter not into the path of the wicked, and walk not in the way of evil men.

פְּרָעֵהוּ אַל-תַּעֲבָר-בּוֹ; שְׂטֵה מֵעָלָיו וַעֲבֹר
pera'ehu al-ta'avar-bo; seteh me'alav va'avor
Avoid it, pass not by it; turn from it, and pass on.

כִּי לֹא יִשְׁנוּ, אִם-לֹא יָרֵעוּ; וְנִגְזְלָה שְׁנָתָם, אִם-לֹא יַכְשִׁילוּ
ki lo yishnu im-lo yare'u; venigzelah shenatam, im-lo yachshilu
For they sleep not, except they have done evil; and their sleep is taken away, unless they cause some to fall.

כִּי לָחֲמוּ, לֶחֶם רֶשַׁע; וְיֵין חֲמָסִים יִשְׁתּוּ
ki lachamu lechem resha'; veyein chamasim yishtu
For they eat the bread of wickedness, and drink the wine of violence.

וְאֹרַח צַדִּיקִים, כְּאוֹר נֹגַהּ: הוֹלֵךְ וָאוֹר, עַד-נְכוֹן הַיּוֹם
ve'orach tzaddikim ke'or nogah; holech va'or, ad-nechon hayom
But the path of the righteous is as the light of dawn, that shineth more and more unto the perfect day.

דֶּרֶךְ רְשָׁעִים, כָּאֲפֵלָה: לֹא יָדְעוּ, בַּמֶּה יִכָּשֵׁלוּ
derech resha'im ka'afelah; lo yade'u, bammeh yikkashelu
The way of the wicked is as darkness; they know not at what they stumble.

בְּנִי, לִדְבָרַי הַקְשִׁיבָה; לַאֲמָרַי, הַט-אָזְנֶךָ
beni lidvarai hakshivah; la'amarai, hat-'ozenecha
My son, attend to my words; incline thine ear unto my sayings.

אַל-יַלִּיזוּ מֵעֵינֶיךָ; שָׁמְרֵם, בְּתוֹךְ לְבָבֶךָ
'al-yallizu me'eineicha; shomerem, betoch levavecha
Let them not depart from thine eyes; keep them in the midst of thy heart.

כִּי-חַיִּים הֵם, לְמֹצְאֵיהֶם; וּלְכָל-בְּשָׂרוֹ מַרְפֵּא
ki-chayim hem lemotze'eihem; ulechol-besaro marpe
For they are life unto those that find them, and health to all their flesh.

מִכָּל-מִשְׁמָר, נְצֹר לִבֶּךָ: כִּי-מִמֶּנּוּ, תּוֹצְאוֹת חַיִּים
mikkol-mishmar netzor libbecha; ki-mimmennu, totze'ot chayim
Above all that thou guardest keep thy heart; for out of it are the issues of life.

ד

שִׁמְעוּ בָנִים, מוּסַר אָב; וְהַקְשִׁיבוּ, לָדַעַת בִּינָה
Shim'u vanim musar av; vehakshivu, lada'at binah
Hear, ye children, the instruction of a father, and attend to know understanding.

כִּי לֶקַח טוֹב, נָתַתִּי לָכֶם; תּוֹרָתִי, אַל-תַּעֲזֹבוּ
ki lekach tov natatti lachem; torati, al-ta'azovu
For I give you good doctrine; forsake ye not my teaching.

כִּי-בֵן, הָיִיתִי לְאָבִי; רַךְ וְיָחִיד, לִפְנֵי אִמִּי
ki-ven hayiti le'avi; rach veyachid, lifnei immi
For I was a son unto my father, tender and an only one in the sight of my mother.

וַיֹּרֵנִי--וַיֹּאמֶר לִי, יִתְמָךְ-דְּבָרַי לִבֶּךָ; שְׁמֹר מִצְוֹתַי וֶחְיֵה
vayoreni, vayomer li, yitmoch-devarai libbecha; shemor mitzvotai vechyeh
And he taught me, and said unto me: 'Let thy heart hold fast my words, keep my commandments, and live;

קְנֵה חָכְמָה, קְנֵה בִינָה; אַל-תִּשְׁכַּח וְאַל-תֵּט, מֵאִמְרֵי-פִי
keneh chochmah keneh vinah; al-tishkach ve'al-tet, me'imrei-fi
Get wisdom, get understanding; forget not, neither decline from the words of my mouth;

אַל-תַּעַזְבֶהָ וְתִשְׁמְרֶךָּ; אֱהָבֶהָ וְתִצְּרֶךָּ
'al-ta'azveha vetishmereka; ehaveha vetitzereka
Forsake her not, and she will preserve thee; love her, and she will keep thee.

רֵאשִׁית חָכְמָה, קְנֵה חָכְמָה; וּבְכָל-קִנְיָנְךָ, קְנֵה בִינָה
reshit chochmah keneh chochmah uvechol-kinyanecha, keneh vinah
The beginning of wisdom is: Get wisdom; yea, with all thy getting get understanding.

סַלְסְלֶהָ וּתְרוֹמְמֶךָּ; תְּכַבֵּדְךָ, כִּי תְחַבְּקֶנָּה
salseleha uteromemeka; techabbedecha, ki techabbekennah
Extol her, and she will exalt thee; she will bring thee to honour, when thou dost embrace her.

תִּתֵּן לְרֹאשְׁךָ, לִוְיַת-חֵן; עֲטֶרֶת תִּפְאֶרֶת תְּמַגְּנֶךָּ
titten leroshecha livyat-chen; ateret tif'eret temaggeneka
She will give to thy head a chaplet of grace; a crown of glory will she bestow on thee.'

שְׁמַע בְּנִי, וְקַח אֲמָרָי; וְיִרְבּוּ לְךָ, שְׁנוֹת חַיִּים
shema beni vekach amarai; veyirbu lecha, shenot chayim
Hear, O my son, and receive my sayings; and the years of thy life shall be many.

בְּדֶרֶךְ חָכְמָה, הֹרֵיתִיךָ; הִדְרַכְתִּיךָ, בְּמַעְגְּלֵי-יֹשֶׁר
bederech chochmah horeticha; hidrachticha, bema'gelei-yosher
I have taught thee in the way of wisdom; I have led thee in paths of uprightness.

אִם-תִּשְׁכַּב לֹא-תִפְחָד; וְשָׁכַבְתָּ, וְעָרְבָה שְׁנָתֶךָ

'im-tishkav lo-tifchad; veshachavta, ve'arevah shenatecha

When thou liest down, thou shalt not be afraid; yea, thou shalt lie down, and thy sleep shall be sweet.

אַל-תִּירָא, מִפַּחַד פִּתְאֹם; וּמִשֹּׁאַת רְשָׁעִים, כִּי תָבֹא

'al-tira mippachad pit'om; umisho'at resha'im, ki tavo

Be not afraid of sudden terror, neither of the destruction of the wicked, when it cometh;

כִּי-יְהוָה, יִהְיֶה בְכִסְלֶךָ; וְשָׁמַר רַגְלְךָ מִלָּכֶד

ki-hashem yihyeh vechislecha; veshamar raglecha millached

For the LORD will be thy confidence, and will keep thy foot from being caught.

אַל-תִּמְנַע-טוֹב מִבְּעָלָיו--בִּהְיוֹת לְאֵל יָדְךָ לַעֲשׂוֹת

'al-timna'-tov mibbe'alav; bihyot le'el yadecha la'asot

Withhold not good from him to whom it is due, when it is in the power of thy hand to do it.

אַל-תֹּאמַר לְרֵעֲךָ, לֵךְ וָשׁוּב--וּמָחָר אֶתֵּן; וְיֵשׁ אִתָּךְ

'al-tomar lere'acha lech vashuv umachar etten, veyesh ittach

Say not unto thy neighbour: 'Go, and come again, and to-morrow I will give'; when thou hast it by thee.

אַל-תַּחֲרֹשׁ עַל-רֵעֲךָ רָעָה; וְהוּא-יוֹשֵׁב לָבֶטַח אִתָּךְ

'al-tacharosh al-re'acha ra'ah; vehu-yoshev lavetach ittach

Devise not evil against thy neighbour, seeing he dwelleth securely by thee.

אַל-תָּרִיב עִם-אָדָם חִנָּם--אִם-לֹא גְמָלְךָ רָעָה

al-tariv im-'adam chinnam; im-lo gemalecha ra'ah

Strive not with a man without cause, if he have done thee no harm.

אַל-תְּקַנֵּא, בְּאִישׁ חָמָס; וְאַל-תִּבְחַר, בְּכָל-דְּרָכָיו

'al-tekannei be'ish chamas; ve'al-tivchar, bechol-derachav

Envy thou not the man of violence, and choose none of his ways.

כִּי תוֹעֲבַת יְהוָה נָלוֹז; וְאֶת-יְשָׁרִים סוֹדוֹ

ki to'avat hashem naloz; ve'et-yesharim sodo

For the perverse is an abomination to the LORD; but His counsel is with the upright.

מְאֵרַת יְהוָה, בְּבֵית רָשָׁע; וּנְוֵה צַדִּיקִים יְבָרֵךְ

me'erat hashem beveit rasha'; uneveh tzaddikim yevarech

The curse of the LORD is in the house of the wicked; but He blesseth the habitation of the righteous.

אִם-לַלֵּצִים הוּא-יָלִיץ; וְלַעֲנָוִים, יִתֶּן-חֵן

'im-lalletzim hu-yalitz; vela'anavim, yitten-chen

If it concerneth the scorners, He scorneth them, but unto the humble He giveth grace.

כָּבוֹד, חֲכָמִים יִנְחָלוּ; וּכְסִילִים, מֵרִים קָלוֹן

kavod chachamim yinchalu; uchesilim, merim kalon

The wise shall inherit honour; but as for the fools, they carry away shame.

כִּי אֶת אֲשֶׁר יֶאֱהַב יְהוָה יוֹכִיחַ; וּכְאָב, אֶת-בֵּן יִרְצֶה

ki et asher ye'ehav hashem yochiach; uche'av, et-ben yirtzeh

For whom the LORD loveth He correcteth, even as a father the son in whom he delighteth.

.אַשְׁרֵי אָדָם, מָצָא חָכְמָה; וְאָדָם, יָפִיק תְּבוּנָה

'ashrei adam matza chochmah ve'adam, yafik tevunah

Happy is the man that findeth wisdom, and the man that obtaineth understanding.

כִּי טוֹב סַחְרָהּ, מִסְּחַר-כָּסֶף; וּמֵחָרוּץ, תְּבוּאָתָהּ

ki tov sachrah missechar-kasef; umecharutz, tevu'atah

For the merchandise of it is better than the merchandise of silver, and the gain thereof than fine gold.

יְקָרָה הִיא, מִפְּנִינִים; וְכָל-חֲפָצֶיךָ, לֹא יִשְׁווּ-בָהּ

yekarah hi mippeninim; vechol-chafatzeicha, lo yishvu-vah

She is more precious than rubies; and all the things thou canst desire are not to be compared unto her.

אֹרֶךְ יָמִים, בִּימִינָהּ; בִּשְׂמֹאולָהּ, עֹשֶׁר וְכָבוֹד

'orech yamim biyminah; bismolah, osher vechavod

Length of days is in her right hand; in her left hand are riches and honour.

דְּרָכֶיהָ דַרְכֵי-נֹעַם; וְכָל-נְתִיבוֹתֶיהָ שָׁלוֹם

deracheiha darchei-no'am; vechol-netivoteiha shalom

Her ways are ways of pleasantness, and all her paths are peace.

עֵץ-חַיִּים הִיא, לַמַּחֲזִיקִים בָּהּ; וְתֹמְכֶיהָ מְאֻשָּׁר

'etz-chayim hi lammachazikim bah; vetomcheiha me'ushar

She is a tree of life to them that lay hold upon her, and happy is every one that holdest her fast.

יְהוָה--בְּחָכְמָה יָסַד-אָרֶץ; כּוֹנֵן שָׁמַיִם, בִּתְבוּנָה

hashem bechochmah yasad-'aretz; konen shamayim, bitvunah

The LORD by wisdom founded the earth; by understanding He established the heavens.

בְּדַעְתּוֹ, תְּהוֹמוֹת נִבְקָעוּ; וּשְׁחָקִים, יִרְעֲפוּ-טָל

beda'to tehomot nivka'u; ushechakim, yir'afu-tal

By His knowledge the depths were broken up, and the skies drop down the dew.

בְּנִי, אַל-יָלֻזוּ מֵעֵינֶיךָ; נְצֹר תֻּשִׁיָּה, וּמְזִמָּה

beni al-yaluzu me'eineicha; netzor tushiyah, umezimmah

My son, let not them depart from thine eyes; keep sound wisdom and discretion;

וְיִהְיוּ חַיִּים לְנַפְשֶׁךָ; וְחֵן, לְגַרְגְּרֹתֶיךָ

veyihyu chayim lenafshecha; vechen, legargeroteicha

So shall they be life unto thy soul, and grace to thy neck.

אָז תֵּלֵךְ לָבֶטַח דַּרְכֶּךָ; וְרַגְלְךָ, לֹא תִגּוֹף

'az telech lavetach darkecha; veraglecha, lo tiggof

Then shalt thou walk in thy way securely, and thou shalt not dash thy foot.

ג

בְּנִי, תּוֹרָתִי אַל-תִּשְׁכָּח; וּמִצְוֹתַי, יִצֹּר לִבֶּךָ
Beni torati al-tishkach; umitzvotai, yitzor libbecha
My son, forget not my teaching; but let thy heart keep my commandments;

כִּי אֹרֶךְ יָמִים, וּשְׁנוֹת חַיִּים--וְשָׁלוֹם, יוֹסִיפוּ לָךְ
ki orech yamim ushenot chayim; veshalom, yosifu lach
For length of days, and years of life, and peace, will they add to thee.

חֶסֶד וֶאֱמֶת, אַל-יַעַזְבֻךָ: קָשְׁרֵם עַל-גַּרְגְּרוֹתֶיךָ; כָּתְבֵם, עַל-לוּחַ לִבֶּךָ
chesed ve'emet, al-ya'azvucha kosherem al-gargeroteicha; kotevem, al-luach libbecha
Let not kindness and truth forsake thee; bind them about thy neck, write them upon the table of thy heart;

וּמְצָא-חֵן וְשֵׂכֶל-טוֹב--בְּעֵינֵי אֱלֹהִים וְאָדָם
umetza-chen vesechel-tov; be'einei elohim ve'adam
So shalt thou find grace and good favour in the sight of God and man.

בְּטַח אֶל-יְהוָה, בְּכָל-לִבֶּךָ; וְאֶל-בִּינָתְךָ, אַל-תִּשָּׁעֵן
betach el-hashem bechol-libbecha; ve'el-binatcha, al-tisha'en
Trust in the LORD with all thy heart, and lean not upon thine own understanding.

בְּכָל-דְּרָכֶיךָ דָעֵהוּ; וְהוּא, יְיַשֵּׁר אֹרְחֹתֶיךָ
bechol-deracheicha da'ehu; vehu, yeyasher orchoteicha
In all thy ways acknowledge Him, and He will direct thy paths.

אַל-תְּהִי חָכָם בְּעֵינֶיךָ; יְרָא אֶת-יְהוָה, וְסוּר מֵרָע
'al-tehi chacham be'eineicha; yera et-hashem vesur mera
Be not wise in thine own eyes; fear the LORD, and depart from evil;

רִפְאוּת, תְּהִי לְשָׁרֶּךָ; וְשִׁקּוּי, לְעַצְמוֹתֶיךָ
rif'ut tehi lesharrecha; veshikkui, le'atzmoteicha
It shall be health to thy navel, and marrow to thy bones.

כַּבֵּד אֶת-יְהוָה, מֵהוֹנֶךָ; וּמֵרֵאשִׁית, כָּל-תְּבוּאָתֶךָ
kabbed et-hashem mehonecha; umereshit, kol-tevu'atecha
Honour the LORD with thy substance, and with the first-fruits of all thine increase;

וְיִמָּלְאוּ אֲסָמֶיךָ שָׂבָע; וְתִירוֹשׁ, יְקָבֶיךָ יִפְרֹצוּ
veyimmale'u asameicha sava'; vetirosh, yekaveicha yifrotzu
So shall thy barns be filled with plenty, and thy vats shall overflow with new wine.

מוּסַר יְהוָה, בְּנִי אַל-תִּמְאָס; וְאַל-תָּקֹץ, בְּתוֹכַחְתּוֹ
musar hashem beni al-tim'as; ve'al-takotz, betochachto
My son, despise not the chastening of the LORD, neither spurn thou His correction;

לְהַצִּילְךָ, מִדֶּרֶךְ רָע; מֵאִישׁ, מְדַבֵּר תַּהְפֻּכוֹת

lehatzilecha midderech ra'; me'ish, medabber tahpuchot

To deliver thee from the way of evil, from the men that speak froward things;

הַעֹזְבִים, אָרְחוֹת יֹשֶׁר--לָלֶכֶת, בְּדַרְכֵי-חֹשֶׁךְ

ha'ozevim orechot yosher; lalechet, bedarchei-choshech

Who leave the paths of uprightness, to walk in the ways of darkness;

הַשְּׂמֵחִים, לַעֲשׂוֹת רָע; יָגִילוּ, בְּתַהְפֻּכוֹת רָע

hassemechim la'asot ra'; yagilu, betahpuchot ra

Who rejoice to do evil, and delight in the frowardness of evil;

אֲשֶׁר אָרְחֹתֵיהֶם עִקְּשִׁים; וּנְלוֹזִים, בְּמַעְגְּלוֹתָם

'asher orechoteihem ikkeshim; unelozim, bema'gelotam

Who are crooked in their ways, and perverse in their paths;

לְהַצִּילְךָ, מֵאִשָּׁה זָרָה; מִנָּכְרִיָּה, אֲמָרֶיהָ הֶחֱלִיקָה

lehatzilecha me'ishah zarah; minnocheriyah, amareiha hechelikah

To deliver thee from the strange woman, even from the alien woman that maketh smooth her words;

הַעֹזֶבֶת, אַלּוּף נְעוּרֶיהָ; וְאֶת-בְּרִית אֱלֹהֶיהָ שָׁכֵחָה

ha'ozevet alluf ne'ureiha; ve'et-berit eloheiha shachechah

That forsaketh the lord of her youth, and forgetteth the covenant of her God.

כִּי שָׁחָה אֶל-מָוֶת בֵּיתָהּ; וְאֶל-רְפָאִים, מַעְגְּלֹתֶיהָ

ki shachah el-mavet beitah; ve'el-refa'im, ma'geloteiha

For her house sinketh down unto death, and her paths unto the shades;

כָּל-בָּאֶיהָ, לֹא יְשׁוּבוּן; וְלֹא-יַשִּׂיגוּ, אָרְחוֹת חַיִּים

kol-ba'eiha lo yeshuvun; velo-yassigu, orechot chayim

None that go unto her return, neither do they attain unto the paths of life;

לְמַעַן--תֵּלֵךְ, בְּדֶרֶךְ טוֹבִים; וְאָרְחוֹת צַדִּיקִים תִּשְׁמֹר

lema'an, telech bederech tovim; ve'orechot tzaddikim tishmor

That thou mayest walk in the way of good men, and keep the paths of the righteous.

כִּי-יְשָׁרִים יִשְׁכְּנוּ-אָרֶץ; וּתְמִימִים, יִוָּתְרוּ בָהּ

ki-yesharim yishkenu-'aretz; utemimim, yivvateru vah

For the upright shall dwell in the land, and the whole-hearted shall remain in it.

וּרְשָׁעִים, מֵאֶרֶץ יִכָּרֵתוּ; וּבוֹגְדִים, יִסְּחוּ מִמֶּנָּה

uresha'im me'eretz yikkaretu; uvogedim, yissechu mimmennah

But the wicked shall be cut off from the land, and the faithless shall be plucked up out of it.

ב

בְּנִי, אִם-תִּקַּח אֲמָרָי; וּמִצְוֺתַי, תִּצְפֹּן אִתָּךְ
Beni im-tikkach amarai; umitzvotai, titzpon ittach
My son, if thou wilt receive my words, and lay up my commandments with thee;

לְהַקְשִׁיב לַחָכְמָה אָזְנֶךָ; תַּטֶּה לִבְּךָ, לַתְּבוּנָה
lehakshiv lachachemah ozenecha; tatteh libbecha, lattevunah
So that thou make thine ear attend unto wisdom, and thy heart incline to discernment;

כִּי אִם לַבִּינָה תִקְרָא; לַתְּבוּנָה, תִּתֵּן קוֹלֶךָ
ki im labbinah tikra; lattevunah, titten kolecha
Yea, if thou call for understanding, and lift up thy voice for discernment;

אִם-תְּבַקְשֶׁנָּה כַכָּסֶף; וְכַמַּטְמוֹנִים תַּחְפְּשֶׂנָּה
'im-tevakshennah chakkasef; vechammatmonim tachpesennah
If thou seek her as silver, and search for her as for hid treasures;

אָז--תָּבִין, יִרְאַת יְהוָה; וְדַעַת אֱלֹהִים תִּמְצָא
'az, tavin yir'at hashem veda'at elohim timtza
Then shalt thou understand the fear of the LORD, and find the knowledge of God.

כִּי-יְהוָה, יִתֵּן חָכְמָה; מִפִּיו, דַּעַת וּתְבוּנָה
ki-hashem yitten chochmah mippiv, da'at utevunah
For the LORD giveth wisdom, out of His mouth cometh knowledge and discernment;

יִצְפֹּן לַיְשָׁרִים, תּוּשִׁיָּה; מָגֵן, לְהֹלְכֵי תֹם
yitzpon laysharim tushiyah; magen, leholechei tom
He layeth up sound wisdom for the upright, He is a shield to them that walk in integrity;

לִנְצֹר, אָרְחוֹת מִשְׁפָּט; וְדֶרֶךְ חֲסִידָו יִשְׁמֹר
lintzor arechot mishpat; vederech chasidav yishmor
That He may guard the paths of justice, and preserve the way of His godly ones.

אָז--תָּבִין, צֶדֶק וּמִשְׁפָּט; וּמֵישָׁרִים, כָּל-מַעְגַּל-טוֹב
'az, tavin tzedek umishpat; umeisharim, kol-ma'gal-tov
Then shalt thou understand righteousness and justice, and equity, yea, every good path.

כִּי-תָבוֹא חָכְמָה בְלִבֶּךָ; וְדַעַת, לְנַפְשְׁךָ יִנְעָם
ki-tavo chochmah velibbecha; veda'at, lenafshecha yin'am
For wisdom shall enter into thy heart, and knowledge shall be pleasant unto thy soul;

מְזִמָּה, תִּשְׁמֹר עָלֶיךָ; תְּבוּנָה תִנְצְרֶכָּה
mezimmah tishmor aleicha, tevunah tintzerekkah
Discretion shall watch over thee, discernment shall guard thee;

תָּשׁוּבוּ, לְתוֹכַחְתִּי: הִנֵּה אַבִּיעָה לָכֶם רוּחִי; אוֹדִיעָה דְבָרַי אֶתְכֶם
tashuvu, letochachti hinneh abbi'ah lachem ruchi; odi'ah devarai etchem
Turn you at my reproof; behold, I will pour out my spirit unto you, I will make known my words unto you.

יַעַן קָרָאתִי, וַתְּמָאֵנוּ; נָטִיתִי יָדִי, וְאֵין מַקְשִׁיב
ya'an karati vattema'enu; natiti yadi, ve'ein makshiv
Because I have called, and ye refused, I have stretched out my hand, and no man attended,

וַתִּפְרְעוּ כָל-עֲצָתִי; וְתוֹכַחְתִּי, לֹא אֲבִיתֶם
vattifre'u chol-'atzati; vetochachti, lo avitem
But ye have set at nought all my counsel, and would none of my reproof;

גַּם-אֲנִי, בְּאֵידְכֶם אֶשְׂחָק; אֶלְעַג, בְּבֹא פַחְדְּכֶם
gam-'ani be'eidechem eschak; el'ag, bevo fachdechem
I also, in your calamity, will laugh, I will mock when your dread cometh;

בְּבֹא כְשׁוֹאָה, פַּחְדְּכֶם--וְאֵידְכֶם, כְּסוּפָה יֶאֱתֶה
bevo chesho'ah pachdechem, ve'eidechem kesufah ye'eteh
When your dread cometh as a storm, and your calamity cometh on as a whirlwind;

בְּבֹא עֲלֵיכֶם, צָרָה וְצוּקָה
bevo aleichem, tzarah vetzukah
when trouble and distress come upon you.

אָז יִקְרָאֻנְנִי, וְלֹא אֶעֱנֶה; יְשַׁחֲרֻנְנִי, וְלֹא יִמְצָאֻנְנִי
'az yikra'uneni velo e'eneh; yeshacharuneni, velo yimtza'uneni
Then will they call me, but I will not answer, they will seek me earnestly, but they shall not find me.

תַּחַת, כִּי-שָׂנְאוּ דָעַת; וְיִרְאַת יְהוָה, לֹא בָחָרוּ
tachat ki-sane'u da'at; veyir'at hashem lo vacharu
For that they hated knowledge, and did not choose the fear of the LORD;

לֹא-אָבוּ לַעֲצָתִי; נָאֲצוּ, כָּל-תּוֹכַחְתִּי
lo-'avu la'atzati; na'atzu, kol-tochachti
They would none of my counsel, they despised all my reproof.

וְיֹאכְלוּ, מִפְּרִי דַרְכָּם; וּמִמֹּעֲצֹתֵיהֶם יִשְׂבָּעוּ
veyochelu mipperi darkam; umimmo'atzoteihem yisba'u
Therefore shall they eat of the fruit of their own way, and be filled with their own devices.

כִּי מְשׁוּבַת פְּתָיִם תַּהַרְגֵם; וְשַׁלְוַת כְּסִילִים תְּאַבְּדֵם
ki meshuvat petayim tahargem; veshalvat kesilim te'abbedem
For the waywardness of the thoughtless shall slay them, and the confidence of fools shall destroy them.

וְשֹׁמֵעַ לִי, יִשְׁכָּן-בֶּטַח; וְשַׁאֲנַן, מִפַּחַד רָעָה
veshomea li yishkon-betach; vesha'anan, mippachad ra'ah
But whoso hearkeneth unto me shall dwell securely, and shall be quiet without fear of evil.'

נִבְלָעֵם, כִּשְׁאוֹל חַיִּים; וּתְמִימִים, כְּיוֹרְדֵי בוֹר

nivla'em kish'ol chayim; utemimim, keyoredei vor

Let us swallow them up alive as the grave, and whole, as those that go down into the pit;

כָּל-הוֹן יָקָר נִמְצָא; נְמַלֵּא בָתֵּינוּ שָׁלָל

kol-hon yakar nimtza; nemallei vatteinu shalal

We shall find all precious substance, we shall fill our houses with spoil;

גּוֹרָלְךָ, תַּפִּיל בְּתוֹכֵנוּ; כִּיס אֶחָד, יִהְיֶה לְכֻלָּנוּ

goralcha tappil betochenu; kis echad, yihyeh lechullanu

Cast in thy lot among us; let us all have one purse'--

בְּנִי--אַל-תֵּלֵךְ בְּדֶרֶךְ אִתָּם; מְנַע רַגְלְךָ, מִנְּתִיבָתָם

beni, al-telech bederech ittam; mena raglecha, minnetivatam

My son, walk not thou in the way with them, restrain thy foot from their path;

כִּי רַגְלֵיהֶם, לָרַע יָרוּצוּ; וִימַהֲרוּ, לִשְׁפָּךְ-דָּם

ki ragleihem lara yarutzu; vimaharu, lishpoch-dam

For their feet run to evil, and they make haste to shed blood.

כִּי-חִנָּם, מְזֹרָה הָרָשֶׁת--בְּעֵינֵי, כָל-בַּעַל כָּנָף

ki-chinnam mezorah harashet; be'einei, chol-ba'al kanaf

For in vain the net is spread in the eyes of any bird;

וְהֵם, לְדָמָם יֶאֱרֹבוּ; יִצְפְּנוּ, לְנַפְשֹׁתָם

vehem ledamam ye'erovu; yitzpenu, lenafshotam

And these lie in wait for their own blood, they lurk for their own lives.

כֵּן--אָרְחוֹת, כָּל-בֹּצֵעַ בָּצַע; אֶת-נֶפֶשׁ בְּעָלָיו יִקָּח

ken, orechot kol-botzea batza'; et-nefesh be'alav yikkach

So are the ways of every one that is greedy of gain; it taketh away the life of the owners thereof.

חָכְמוֹת, בַּחוּץ תָּרֹנָּה; בָּרְחֹבוֹת, תִּתֵּן קוֹלָהּ

chachemot bachutz taronnah; barechovot, titten kolah

Wisdom crieth aloud in the streets, she uttereth her voice in the broad places;

בְּרֹאשׁ הֹמִיּוֹת, תִּקְרָא: בְּפִתְחֵי שְׁעָרִים בָּעִיר--אֲמָרֶיהָ תֹאמֵר

berosh homiyot, tikra befitchei she'arim ba'ir, amareiha tomer

She calleth at the head of the noisy streets, at the entrances of the gates, in the city, she uttereth her words:

עַד-מָתַי, פְּתָיִם--תְּאֵהֲבוּ-פֶתִי

'ad-matai petayim te'ehavu feti

'How long, ye thoughtless, will ye love thoughtlessness?

וְלֵצִים--לָצוֹן, חָמְדוּ לָהֶם; וּכְסִילִים, יִשְׂנְאוּ-דָעַת

veletzim, latzon chamedu lahem; uchesilim, yisne'u-da'at

And how long will scorners delight them in scorning, and fools hate knowledge?

*Remember: Hebrew is Read from <u>Right to Left</u>
מִשְׁלֵי א

מִשְׁלֵי, שְׁלֹמֹה בֶן-דָּוִד--מֶלֶךְ, יִשְׂרָאֵל
Mishlei shelomoh ven-david; melech, yisra'el
The proverbs of Solomon the son of David, king of Israel;

לָדַעַת חָכְמָה וּמוּסָר; לְהָבִין, אִמְרֵי בִינָה
lada'at chochmah umusar; lehavin, imrei vinah
To know wisdom and instruction; to comprehend the words of understanding;

לָקַחַת, מוּסַר הַשְׂכֵּל; צֶדֶק וּמִשְׁפָּט, וּמֵשָׁרִים
lakachat musar haskel; tzedek umishpat, umeisharim
To receive the discipline of wisdom, justice, and right, and equity;

לָתֵת לִפְתָאיִם עָרְמָה; לְנַעַר, דַּעַת וּמְזִמָּה
latet liftayim oremah; lena'ar, da'at umezimmah
To give prudence to the simple, to the young man knowledge and discretion;

יִשְׁמַע חָכָם, וְיוֹסֶף לֶקַח; וְנָבוֹן, תַּחְבֻּלוֹת יִקְנֶה
yishma chachom veyosef lekach; venavon, tachbulot yikneh
That the wise man may hear, and increase in learning, and the man of understanding may attain unto wise counsels;

לְהָבִין מָשָׁל, וּמְלִיצָה; דִּבְרֵי חֲכָמִים, וְחִידֹתָם
lehavin mashol umelitzah; divrei chachamim, vechidotam
To understand a proverb, and a figure; the words of the wise, and their dark sayings.

יִרְאַת יְהוָה, רֵאשִׁית דָּעַת; חָכְמָה וּמוּסָר, אֱוִילִים בָּזוּ
yir'at hashem reshit da'at; chochmah umusar, evilim bazu
The fear of the LORD is the beginning of knowledge; but the foolish despise wisdom and discipline.

שְׁמַע בְּנִי, מוּסַר אָבִיךָ; וְאַל-תִּטֹּשׁ, תּוֹרַת אִמֶּךָ
shema beni musar avicha; ve'al-tittosh, torat immecha
Hear, my son, the instruction of thy father, and forsake not the teaching of thy mother;

כִּי, לִוְיַת חֵן הֵם לְרֹאשֶׁךָ; וַעֲנָקִים, לְגַרְגְּרֹתֶךָ
ki livyat chen hem leroshecha; va'anakim, legargeroteicha
For they shall be a chaplet of grace unto thy head, and chains about thy neck.

בְּנִי-אִם-יְפַתּוּךָ חַטָּאִים, אַל-תֹּבֵא
beni im-yefattucha chatta'im, al-tove
My son, if sinners entice thee, consent thou not.

אִם-יֹאמְרוּ, לְכָה אִתָּנוּ: נֶאֶרְבָה לְדָם; נִצְפְּנָה לְנָקִי חִנָּם
'im-yomeru lechah ittanu ne'ervah ledam; nitzpenah lenaki chinnam
If they say: 'Come with us, let us lie in wait for blood, let us lurk for the innocent without cause;

Hebrew		Vowel		Number	
א	A	אַ	ah	א	1
ב	V	אַ	ah	ב	2
בּ	B	אֶ	ah	ג	3
ג	G	אָה	ah	ד	4
ד	D	אֵ	ei	ה	5
ה	H	אֶ	e	ו	6
ו	V	אֱ	e	ז	7
ז	Z	אֵי	ei	ח	8
ח	KH	אִ	ee	ט	9
ט	T	אִי	ee		
י	Y	אֹ	oh	י	10
כּ	KH	אָ	oh	יא	11
כ	K	אָ	oh	יב	12
ל	L	אוֹ	oh	יג	13
מ	M	אֻ	oo	יד	14
מ	M	אוּ	oo	טו	15
נ	N	אְ	e	טז	16
נ	N			יז	17
ס	S			יח	18
ע	A			יט	19
פּ	F				
פ	P			כ	20
צ	TS			ל	30
ק	K				
ר	R				
שׁ	SH				
שׂ	S				
ת	T				

hebrew audio available:

at

hebrewaudiobible.com

מִשְׁלֵי
Mishlei
Proverbs

Made in the USA
Las Vegas, NV
05 January 2023

65000932R00046